Stalin

A Beginner's Guide

ONEWORLD BEGINNER'S GUIDES combine an original, inventive, and engaging approach with expert analysis on subjects ranging from art and history to religion and politics, and everything in-between. Innovative and affordable, books in the series are perfect for anyone curious about the way the world works and the big ideas of our time.

Stalin

A Beginner's Guide

Abraham Ascher

ONEWORLD

A Oneworld Paperback

First published in North America, Great Britain and Australia by
Oneworld Publications, 2017

ISBN 978-1-78074-913-6
eISBN 978-1-78074-914-3

Typeset by Silicon Chips
Printed and bound in Great Britain by Clays Ltd, St Ives plc

Oneworld Publications
10 Bloomsbury Street
London WC1B 3SR
England

For Anna

Contents

Contents

Acknowledgements

I have been fortunate to have had the advice of several people in writing this biography of Stalin. My wife, who is a professional editor, read the manuscript and, as always, made valuable suggestions for its improvement. At Oneworld, I received very helpful comments from two editors: Sam Carter was the first editor to read a draft of the manuscript and his words of encouragement led me to continue working on it. Shadi Doostdar, the editor who was in charge of the manuscript during the critical period when I revised it, gave me advice that was invariably perceptive and that prompted me to make further improvements. Finally, I want to thank David Inglesfield, the copy-editor, who read the manuscript with great care and made numerous suggestions that made my work more readable.

Introduction

Joseph Stalin and Adolf Hitler are widely regarded as two of the most ruthless dictators of the twentieth century. But unlike Hitler, who has been almost universally depicted by professional historians as a fanatic and mass murderer, Stalin has been spared such widespread condemnation and has even been viewed favorably by some distinguished scholars in the West and by a fair number in Russia. For example, shortly after Stalin's death on 5 March 1953, E. H. Carr, author of numerous acclaimed works on the Soviet Union, ended an evaluation of the Soviet ruler by lauding him as a 'great westernizer' for having modernized Russia's economy and for having turned the country into one of the two great world powers. In offering this appraisal of the man, Carr did not even mention the system of domestic terror enacted under Stalin's auspices.

More recently, Eric Hobsbawm, an avowed Marxist considered by many to have been the United Kingdom's greatest historian in the twentieth century, defended Stalin's economic policies even though they exacted a heavy price, the death of millions of innocent citizens. On 24 October 1994, the *Times Literary Supplement* reported in an interview with the historian conducted by Michael Ignatieff, himself a prominent scholar, that after failing to obtain a clear-cut answer from Hobsbawm on how he could justify his long-standing membership of the Communist Party, Ignatieff summed up the historian's comments as follows: 'What that comes down to is saying that had the radiant tomorrow actually been created, the loss of fifteen, twenty million people might have been justified.' Hobsbawm 'immediately, quickly, horribly, said "Yes".'

The failure of historians to treat the two dictators with the same degree of disdain can be attributed in good measure to the different political commitments of Nazi and communist leaders. The Nazis adopted racism as a central doctrine of their program and scoffed at the idea of treating all human beings with respect. By contrast, Soviet leaders were idealists as young men; they committed themselves to the abolition of the autocratic tsarist regime and the overthrow of capitalism, which they wished to replace with a system of rule based on the principles of egalitarianism and respect for the dignity of citizens of the Russian Empire.

Followers of Karl Marx and key proponents of his socialist philosophy, they insisted that Russia was ripe for a proletarian or working-class revolution even though the country had not yet undergone a bourgeois revolution and its economy had not yet fully evolved into an industrial, capitalist system. The Russian Marxists believed that the oppressed masses not only could overturn the tsarist autocracy but also could place power in the hands of the industrial working class – in short, that Russia could bypass the capitalist stage of development and move immediately from monarchical rule and a predominantly agrarian society to a social and political order controlled by representatives of the working class. Marx himself once suggested that such a course of development might be possible, but generally he rejected the likelihood of its taking place in Russia. And virtually all his disciples in the West insisted that socialism could be reached only after capitalism had matured. In any case, no sooner had the revolution against the old order succeeded in Russia than the new leaders created a political system that in some important respects was more autocratic and more brutal in the treatment of the Russian people than that of the Tsars. They contended that the final goal of benign socialism as envisioned by Marx could only be reached when the more industrialized countries in the West underwent a revolution staged by the working class.

Stalin was part of the leadership of the proletarian revolution in Russia, although he was not one of the charismatic or intellectually most sophisticated men at the helm of the Bolshevik party, eventually to be known as the Communist Party, which engineered the seizure of power in November 1917. Yet within eleven years, in 1928, he succeeded in taking over the leadership of the party and in assuming dictatorial power in the Soviet Union, short for Union of Soviet Socialist Republics (or USSR), as the Russian Empire was now called. Stalin's rise to power is a remarkable story indicating the ability of a clever and ruthless intriguer to outsmart rivals generally considered to have a more thorough grasp of Marxism.

A biography of Stalin, then, must grapple with several fundamental questions: how did Stalin, a person committed to the ideal of economic and social equality in a prosperous society, come to embrace an order that drifted far from these ideals? How did a man of Stalin's talents manage to turn the Soviet Union into one of the most influential world powers? Perhaps most puzzling of all, why is there still a substantial residue of goodwill, more in Russia than in the rest of the world, toward a leader who caused so much pain to his own people and who never came close to achieving the idealistic goals he cherished when he became a revolutionary as a young man?

There is yet another difficulty that a biographer of Stalin must confront: the unreliability of so much that has been written by and about the man who ruled the Soviet Union for twenty-four years. Early in his career, Stalin himself acknowledged in a cynical comment that the written word could not always be trusted. In what is generally regarded as his most original contribution to Marxist thought, his essay on the nationality question published in 1913, he wrote the following in denouncing another socialist who had called G.V. Plekhanov, the founder of Russian Marxism, a demagogue: 'Paper will put up with anything that is written on it.' This was one of Stalin's cleverest comments, and it should serve as a warning to all who venture to write on any aspect of the history of the Soviet Union during the years of his rule.

STALIN'S PSEUDONYMS

To enhance his image and, once he became a revolutionary, to evade the police, Stalin adopted so many different names – several dozen according to the historian Stephen Kotkin – that readers of his biography may be forgiven if they succumb to confusion. He was christened in 1879 as Joseph Djugashvili, but even as a youngster he called himself 'Koba', the hero of the Georgian novel *The Patricide* by Alexander Kazbegi. In that novel Koba is depicted as a man of few words who excelled at climbing high mountains and who defied all authority. Joseph continued to favor this name during his early years as a revolutionary, but after several meetings in 1906 and 1907 with Lenin, a man he greatly admired for his toughness, he began, apparently in 1910, to use the name 'Stalin', which is best translated as 'man of steel', precisely the image he wanted to convey to his colleagues, the masses, and eventually to leaders of foreign countries. Occasionally, he still signed letters with 'K' and sometimes with 'Koba Stalin'. But during the Revolution of 1917 he tended to sign letters and documents with 'People's Commissar I. Stalin', a name that increasingly appealed to him because it sounded genuinely Russian, which was important to him. Unable to shed his Georgian accent, he at least had a name that seemed appropriate for a leader of a country that became ever more mindful of its national – that is, Russian – heritage. And after he rose to the position of absolute ruler, 'Stalin' gave him an additional image he cherished, a person unshakable in his convictions and dedicated to turning the Soviet Union into a great power.

Fortunately, reliable sources for a biography of Stalin are now numerous. Stalin's publications and those of his colleagues and rivals as well as Russian newspapers from 1917 to the present are now available in the libraries of most major universities and in some of the larger public libraries. And since the collapse of the Soviet Union in 1991, a substantial amount of archival material of the Soviet era has been available to Russian and Western scholars, several of whom have published books and articles that shed new light on Stalin and Stalinism. Finally, ever since the 1930s historians have produced numerous biographies of Stalin and his lieutenants, and many of them contain valuable information and thoughtful interpretations.

One of the earliest biographies, written by Boris Souvarine, appeared in 1936, and is still valuable for its understanding of communist thought derived from Souvarine's membership of the Communist Party in France, where his family lived after leaving Russia in 1897. Moreover, Souvarine was fluent in Russian and knew many leaders of the Bolshevik movement; consequently his book on Stalin contains information he had obtained from personal contacts. True, he became a sharp critic of Stalin and communism, but there is no evidence that he produced a distorted picture of events in the Soviet Union.

Of course, he did not have access to archival sources that became available to later biographers of Stalin. The bibliography at the end of the present book lists the most prominent works on the Soviet leader written over the past three or four decades, and readers who crave more information on the Soviet Union will find that these books, several of which run to many hundreds of pages, contain the latest available information on the Soviet ruler. They will also discover an interesting variety of interpretations of the man who stood at the helm of the Soviet Union for twenty-four years.

It is worth noting that although Stalin was not a theorist of distinction, the economic, social and political policies that were his handiwork are often described as *Stalinism*, which suggests that once he reached the pinnacle of power in 1929 he had formulated a comprehensive plan for the achievement of socialism. In other words, Stalin imposed on the Soviet Union his own conception of Marxist theory, the basic principle of which was 'socialism in one country' – that Russia, despite its economic backwardness, could on its own create an egalitarian society.

It is conceivable that had one of his opponents in the struggle for power after Lenin's death in 1924 defeated him, he might also have opted for a rapid move toward the final goals of socialism. By the late 1920s the economic reform initiated by Lenin had run its course and if the Soviet Union was to improve the economy and continue to raise the standard of living, far-reaching changes were needed. But it is hard to believe that any of the other leading Bolsheviks – Leon Trotsky, Grigory Zinoviev, Nikolai Bukharin, to mention only a few – would have resorted to the brutalities that characterized Stalin's rule even though all those leaders had sanctioned severe measures against opponents of communist rule in the years from 1917 to 1921. Lenin, who was not known as a softhearted leader, had allowed a fair number of former Marxist colleagues who opposed his government's policies to leave the Soviet Union.

Stalin was *sui generis*; his upbringing, his education, and, most important, his ruthlessness, differed from those of his colleagues in the very top echelon of the Bolshevik party. Paranoid and convinced that only he knew how to lead their country to the final goal of socialism, he had no qualms about eliminating people he feared as his rivals or suspected of being insufficiently supportive. That is why Stalinism cannot be understood without a firm grasp of Stalin as a human being, without insight into his personality. His power in the 1930s was so sweeping that no other approach can explain how he succeeded in retaining absolute power for twenty-four years and in fundamentally reordering Soviet society. Of course, conditions in the Soviet Union and the state of international affairs must be taken into account, but by themselves these factors do not explain Stalin's achievements. By the same token, a study of his biography may not by itself completely answer the question of how he managed to be so successful a leader, but it is an indispensable first step.

1
Stalin's Early Years, 1879–1899

The upbringing of Joseph Djugashvili (he adopted the name Stalin – 'man of steel' – probably in 1910) was rare among leading Russian revolutionaries, most of whom were born into families that belonged either to the middle class, the gentry, and/or the intelligentsia, that is, highly educated people who exercise cultural or political influence. His parents, both of them semi-literate, had been born as serfs in Georgia, a beautiful country in Eurasia that was annexed by Russia in 1801. The poorest people there, the serfs, were laborers forced to work the land owned by a small number of nobles, who saw to it that their workers were not permitted to move elsewhere. The institution of serfdom was abolished in Georgia in 1865, four years later than in other parts of the Russian Empire.

Poverty was not the only hardship that Stalin endured as a youngster. He grew up in a strikingly dysfunctional family, also an important factor in shaping his character and political outlook. He always spoke kindly of his mother, Yekaterina, who was devoted to him, the only one of her four children to survive birth. Deeply religious, she hoped that her son, most probably born on 21 December 1878 in the small town of Gori, Georgia, would join the clergy. Stalin's father, on the other hand, took little interest in religion or the home. A cobbler, he earned enough to support his family but squandered an increasing amount on liquor; and during his frequent bouts of alcoholism the tremors in his hands reduced his efficiency, and hence his earnings. Prone to irascibility, he sometimes beat his wife, and once even tried to strangle her. He was also given to beating his son, who came to loathe his father. The father often did not show up at home for weeks at a time. To support herself and her son, Yekaterina worked as a seamstress and laundress for middle-class families.

The date of his father's death remains unclear. Stalin's daughter, Svetlana, claimed that he died in a drunken brawl in 1890. Other sources indicate that he died much later, in 1909, of cirrhosis of the liver, which is often caused by excessive drinking. Most biographers of Stalin contend that the violence in his family life left a deep impression on him. When he rose to a prominent position in politics, he displayed few inhibitions about resorting to violence to achieve his goals or to silence his enemies, real or imagined.

Physically, Stalin was not appealing. At five feet four or five inches, he is said to have felt uncomfortable in the presence of taller men. After rising to power, he surrounded himself with shorter functionaries. Apparently, one reason that he liked to have Nikita S. Khrushchev – who became the country's leader shortly after Stalin's death – in his inner circle was that he stood at only five feet three inches. Because of an accident or some infection at the age of eight, Stalin developed a stiffness in his right arm that was sufficiently disabling to prevent him from being drafted into the armed services during World War 1. As a child, he was stricken with smallpox, which left his face pockmarked for the rest of his life.

Academically, the young boy was impressive; his analytic abilities were strong and he had an unusually fine memory. He loved reading books and was adept at taking examinations. Until the age of eight or nine he spoke only Georgian, which is completely different from Russian, the required language at local schools. The boy quickly mastered Russian, eventually his preferred language, which he always spoke with a marked Georgian accent. When he had reached the pinnacle of political power, his subordinates were so subservient that they went to great lengths not to correct his mistakes. At the Eighteenth Party Congress in 1939 the dictator mispronounced the name of the People's Commissariat of Agriculture – he called it Narkomzyom instead of Narkomzem. Whenever later speakers at the Congress referred to that office, they deliberately adopted their leader's pronunciation – an interesting and amusing example of the fear Stalin inspired.

Stalin's mother was determined to enroll her son in the Tiflis Theological Seminary in the hope that he would enter the priesthood and rise to the position of bishop, a career that seemed to be within his reach. Not only did he perform outstandingly at school; he was also appropriately devout, rarely missing a mass. The Seminary was a highly regarded institution that could afford to be selective in its admissions, and the young Stalin seemed to be an ideal candidate. It awarded a scholarship to Joseph, enabling him to begin a demanding course of study in August 1894.

GEORGIA

Georgia, where Stalin lived until his early twenties, is a small country of about 4.5 million people located at the intersection of Europe and Asia. Its widely admired terrain is largely mountainous. The country can also boast of a long and rich history. The Georgians adopted Christianity in the fourth century CE, six centuries before Russia, and their language as well as their culture was uniquely their own. By the eleventh century the country had achieved an impressive level of economic and political power. Georgia remained independent until 1801, when it was annexed by Russia, which had conquered several neighboring regions. The invaders replaced local authorities with Russian viceroys, who ruled arbitrarily and sought to impose Russian culture on the Georgians.

But the conquerors' tasks proved to be more challenging than anticipated. As the eighteenth-century author Prince Vakhushti Bagration pointed out, the Georgians were a proud people who did not easily succumb to invaders: '[They are] intelligent, quick-witted, self-centered and lovers of learning ... They lend loyal support to one another, will remember and repay a good turn but will extract retribution for an insult. They ... are headstrong, ambitious, and apt to flatter and to take offense.'

Stalin abandoned Georgian culture after becoming a political activist, but he never fully shed the personal qualities of the people among whom he was raised. Since the collapse of communism the country has been independent, although relations with the Russian Federation remain tense.

In keeping with the government's policy of imposing Russian culture on ethnic minorities throughout the Empire, the Seminary followed the rituals of the Russian Orthodox Church even though most Georgians practiced Georgian Orthodox Christianity. And classroom instruction was in Russian, seen by most local residents as a disparagement of their language. In addition to theology, students took courses in Latin, Greek, Church Slavonic, Russian history, and Russian literature. No modern foreign languages were taught and the sciences were slighted. The authoritarian approach to learning at the Seminary left its mark on Stalin's style of writing and mode of argument for the rest of his life. He was always dogmatic and presented his thoughts crudely; he would pose a question and then answer it in a way that suggested that no alternative response could possibly be correct, just as the pronouncements of the Church were presented as the ultimate truth.

But as a boy of seventeen, Stalin also demonstrated a flair for poetry. He published several poems in the Georgian literary journal *Iveria*. They were marked, in the words of Simon Sebag Montefiore, by 'romantic imagery ... [and] delicacy and purity of rhythm and language'. Apparently, his poems were widely read and even 'became minor Georgian classics'.

As an adult, Stalin claimed that the stifling atmosphere at the Seminary prompted him to take up the revolutionary cause, which may well be the case. In an interview on 13 December

1931, with the German writer Emil Ludwig, Stalin indicated that he became a radical in 'protest against the outrageous regime and the Jesuitical methods prevalent at the seminary'. He granted that the teaching was 'systematic' but insisted that the academic staff was committed to achieving 'sordid ends ... their principal method is spying, prying, worming their way into people's souls and outraging their feelings. What good can there be in that? For instance, the spying in the hostel. At nine o'clock the bell rings for morning tea, we go to the dining room, and when we return to our rooms we find that meantime a search has been made and all our chests have been ransacked.'

Although students who broke the rules were not subjected to physical punishment, discipline was strict. For one thing, the school's rules prescribed what kind of books students were permitted to read. Many novels and all political publications critical of the prevailing order were prohibited. But, as had been true for several decades at the Seminary, many students ignored the official censorship, and it did not take long for Stalin to join a secret circle devoted to socialist literature as well as fiction that dealt with social or political issues. Inspector Father Germogen caught the boy with Victor Hugo's *Ninety-Three*, a work that focused on the French counterrevolutionary events of the Vendée revolt and the Chouannerie. The penalty was severe: a long stay in the 'punishment cell'. Other authors whose works caught the young boy's fancy were Nikolai Nekrasov, Nikolai G. Chernyshevsky, Nikolai Gogol, Emile Zola, and Charles Darwin, to mention only a few. Georgy Elisabetdashvili, one of his friends at the time, recalled that Stalin 'didn't just read books, he *ate* them'. By the time he was seventeen or eighteen, he had read *Kvali*, a weekly journal committed to disseminating the doctrines of Marxism. Of course, none of these works deepened his understanding of theological issues, but that did not faze him. On the contrary, during his first year at the Seminary he began to have doubts about the teachings of Christianity and he drifted toward atheism.

Stalin remained at the Seminary for three more years, but he probably spent more time studying social and political issues than theology. No doubt, even more offensive to the teachers than his participation in the secret circle, he, like many of his class-mates, would pretend during services to be reading prayers while focusing on writings of socialist leaders placed carefully on their knees. In 1897, he received no fewer than nine warnings for vari-ous infractions. On several occasions, he was charged with rude behavior: during prayers, he would talk to other students and laugh out loud, and when he encountered teachers in the halls, he ignored the rule that students must bow to them. It became obvious that the priesthood would not be his calling and in 1899 he left the school under circumstances that are still unclear.

But it is known that at the age of twenty he abandoned his education and became a political activist. His circle of friends regarded him as committed to improving the world but also, despite his sound classical education, as never in doubt about the correctness of his views and unfavorably inclined toward anyone who differed with him. His self-assurance and arrogance served him in good stead in the harsh world of Russian radicalism and eventually in his climb to leadership of the Soviet Union.

Stalin's move in 1899 from student at the Seminary to politi-cal activist made it necessary for him to make some critical deci-sions. Most important, he had to find work to support himself; his mother was not in a position to cover his expenses for a protracted period and probably would not have wanted to because she did not want to make it easy for him to abandon his religious studies. Stalin earned some income by giving lessons to young students and apparently a few former students at the Seminary provided him with financial help. Late in December 1899, he landed a minor, part-time post at the Tiflis Observatory, but his heart was not in that work. He kept busy by spending several hours a week indoctrinating workers in Marxist ideas.

2

A Young Revolutionary, 1899–1917

In seeking to undermine the existing sociopolitical order in Russia and replace it with one committed to socialism, Stalin and his Marxist colleagues faced a task of monumental proportions. Unlike Western Europe and Britain, Russia was still predominantly agricultural early in the twentieth century, with a tiny proletariat numbering not more than three million out of a total population of roughly 150 million. Industrialization on a large scale took hold in the country only in the 1890s, more than a century later than in Great Britain. Although Russia made impressive progress in modernizing the economy, in 1914 it lagged far behind the major powers in Europe. True, it was now the fifth industrial power in the world, but labor productivity and per capita income there rose much more slowly than in Western Europe. In 1910, per capita income amounted to only a third of the average in the industrial sectors of Europe.

Economic conditions of the peasantry, about eighty percent of the total population, were, if anything, even worse. Serfdom had been abolished in 1861, but the lot of the peasants deteriorated in several important respects. For one thing, the rapid growth of the population between 1887 and 1905 resulted in a decline of over twenty percent in the average landholding of peasant households, from 13.2 to 10.4 desiatinas (one desiatina equals 2.7 acres). Production remained abysmally low, in part because the system of communal landownership, which governed about four fifths of the peasants' holdings, was not conducive to long-range planning or to the application of modern farming techniques. Many statistics could be cited to demonstrate the wretched conditions in the countryside, but none is more telling than the following: the death rate of Russia was about double that of England.

Politically and socially, modernization had made few inroads in the country's institutions. The Russian Empire continued to be governed by hereditary monarchs who claimed to possess autocratic power by divine right. Although the rulers stressed that obedience to them was a religious obligation, they did not rely solely on the conscience of the people to follow their commands. The authorities in St. Petersburg also sought to shape public opinion by censoring books, periodicals, and newspapers and, more important, they maintained a system of police surveillance over the citizens and arbitrarily meted out severe punishments (generally exile to distant locations, or imprisonment) to anyone considered 'seditious', a term defined very broadly.

Tsar Nicholas II, who ascended the throne in 1894, possessed none of the qualities necessary for effective leadership. He did not understand that even rulers who claim absolute power need to gain the confidence of large sectors of the population. Although moderately intelligent, he lacked the personal drive and vision to take charge of the government, to familiarize himself with the workings of his administration, and to instill a sense of purpose and direction into the ministers and the bureaucracy. He was narrow-minded and prejudiced, incapable of tolerating people who did not fit into his conception of a true Russian, a fatal flaw in a country composed of over a hundred ethnic groups with a wide range of cultures, languages, and religions; the minorities, moreover, constituted more than half the Empire's population. Nicholas also could not bear the word 'intelligentsia', which he considered 'repulsive' because many of its members tended to oppose autocratic rule. The Tsar was convinced that except for the intelligentsia most people in the Empire were deeply devoted to him.

Although it is true that many ordinary Russians, especially among the peasantry, still revered their ruler, a growing number were becoming increasingly disaffected. This is not surprising: they were no longer serfs, but they were not free citizens. They could not move from one place to another without official permission, and in many respects the government and the land-lords still exercised arbitrary and inhumane control over them. For example, officials could imprison a peasant or exile him to Siberia for alleged violations of the law without a trial. Only in 1903 did the government prohibit corporal punishment of convicted criminals.

It was not until 1906, and much more extensively in 1917, that sizable numbers of peasants engaged in large-scale distur-bances that made them a potent political force in the country-side. Russian Marxists expressed sympathy for the plight of the peasants, but their primary incentive in devoting themselves to revolutionary activism was the desire to improve the lot of the industrial working class, who, they believed, would be the savior of the world from the evils of capitalism, as had been predicted by the German philosopher Karl Marx. In Germany and other Western countries Marx's thesis seemed plausible because the proletariat in the second half of the nineteenth century was already a significant force that had grown rapidly in size and political influence with each advance in industrialization.

In the Russian Empire, however, conditions were radically different. Industrialization on a massive scale took hold only in the 1890s, which meant that early in the twentieth century the country lagged far behind such Western powers as Germany and Great Britain. The proletariat in Russia constituted a much smaller portion of the population, which makes it all the more remark-able that it exerted so powerful an influence in the country's political evolution in 1917. To a considerable degree, this weight resulted from the structure of industrialization in Russia. Because Russian entrepreneurs tended to adopt the form of production and factory organization of economically more advanced countries, industry was highly concentrated, more so even than in Germany and the United States. The considerable size of many factories was a boon to labor organizers and political activists, who could easily reach large numbers of workers resentful of the harsh conditions in the workplace.

Moreover, government officials and industrialists handled the 'labor question' with astonishing insensitivity. Until 1905, they frequently denied that there was such a problem and insisted that relations between employers and their workers were patriarchal in character, comparable to the benevolent relations between landlords and peasants. Consequently, employers asserted that Russian workers would not succumb to the enticements of outside agitators, the alleged fomenters of labor unrest, to demand higher rewards for their labor.

In fact, conditions for factory workers were so grim that they hardly needed to be persuaded to resent their plight. They worked eleven and a half hours a day five days a week and somewhat less on Saturdays. Their wages were exceedingly low, and since many of them returned to their villages for part of the year to till the fields, they were housed in large, unsanitary barracks during their service at the factory. Many owners of industrial plants acted like 'Tsars in their realm' and looked upon their workers as 'servants and slaves'. The laws governing the contractual obligations of workers were precise and stern: according to the Penal Code of 1845, collective resistance to employers was tantamount to an uprising against the state, punishable by fifteen years of hard labor.

A further disadvantage of industrial workers was that they were culturally backward: in 1897, only about fifty percent of them were literate, and many who were classed as literate could barely read and write. Nevertheless, they gradually began to realize that they could take matters into their own hands in seeking to improve their conditions. Between 1862 and 1869, six strikes and twenty-nine 'disturbances' took place; from 1870 to 1885, the average number of annual strikes rose to twenty and the number of disturbances increased from three to twenty-three. During the Revolution of 1905, workers played a critical role in a series of events that on two occasions came close to shaking the foundations of the state. The growing unrest among workers did not signify that many of them understood the subtleties of Marxist doctrine. But at a time of national crisis such as Russia experienced in 1917, resulting from three years of a war that the country was losing, a substantial number among the proletariat followed the lead of Marxist activists who were committed to advancing their interests.

In April 1900, when Stalin was only twenty-one, he took charge of the agitation among railway workers in the Georgian city of Tiflis, many of whom he had come to know while he was still a student. The police found out about this activity and on 1 March 1901 raided the observatory where he had been working. They arrested several of Stalin's colleagues, but since he was not at work he avoided being seized. Not long afterward, he lost his job, freeing him to switch to what he considered his real calling, full-time devotion to the revolutionary cause. As far as we know, several friends from his days at the Seminary covered his living expenses.

Even at this early stage of his career he acquired the reputation of being a schemer. Several party members suspected him of having fomented a plot against Sylvester Jibladze, the local leader of the Social Democrats, apparently in the hope of replacing him. The party organization in Tiflis formed a tribunal to examine the charges against Stalin and, ruling that he was guilty of 'unjust slander', ejected him from the organization.

Among local activists, Stalin was also regarded as difficult to work with, as he was often overbearing and prone to vile fits of temper. Frequently, he insisted on going his own way even if that meant antagonizing his colleagues. These traits remained a central feature of his character throughout his life and should be kept in mind because they will shed light on his behavior years later when he occupied senior positions in the Communist Party.

Stalin's first brush with the police took place in 1902. He had moved to Batumi, on the Black Sea coast of western Georgia, a city with a population of about 200,000 and one of the few areas in Georgia that was making significant progress in industrialization. The rich mineral resources in the region had attracted a considerable number of investors, including the Rothschilds. The city was also a center of oil refining, and eventually various other industries flourished there. Conditions for laborers in the new industries were harsh and, not surprisingly, worker discontent became widespread, making the city an attractive center for Marxist activists. Stalin had moved there early in 1901 and witnessed a strike during which the police fired on workers, killing thirteen and wounding fifty-three in a series of street clashes that came to be known as the Batumi Massacre. The workers were deeply shaken, but Stalin considered the bloodshed a great victory. 'Today,' he told a colleague, 'we advanced several years. We lost comrades but we won.' Stalin urged a young Marxist to publish details of the police action and to be sure to 'thank the mothers who raised such fine sons'. He then sought to avenge the loss of life by planning the assassination of the manager of the Rothschild firm, but the attempt failed.

Having been informed of Stalin's agitation among workers, the police placed him high on their list of activists to be arrested, but for several weeks he managed to evade them by moving from one friendly apartment to another. During the night of 5 April 1901, however, they caught up with him and put him in the local jail. Fellow prisoners were impressed by the young man's composure and his dedication to the revolutionary cause – he spent much of his time reading and writing. But he left enough time each day to work on becoming, in Montefiore's words, the 'king-pin' of the Batumi prison, 'dominating his friends, terrorizing the intellectuals, suborning the guards and befriending the criminals'. The police questioned him about his political activities and those of his comrades, but by responding to all the queries with false or misleading information he revealed nothing of value. Stalin's incarceration in Batumi lasted about a year and was followed by six months' imprisonment in Kutais before he was sentenced to three years of exile in Novaia Uda, an eastern Siberian village in the province of Irkutsk.

During the tsarist era, exile was far from comfortable, but for a revolutionary it was a badge of honour to have been mistreated by the authorities. Actually, the police did not maintain very rigid control over political prisoners. It was not difficult to escape from exile, and within two months Stalin made his way back to Tiflis.

Over the course of eleven years, from 1902 to 1913, Stalin managed to escape from exile no fewer than six times. His last period of exile lasted longer than any previous one, from 1913 to 1917. He left this place of confinement legally because the government that replaced the tsarist regime in March 1917 immediately freed all political exiles. Stalin had not attempted to escape this time because he had been sent to Solvychegodsk, a small town in northern Russia, from which flight was exceedingly hard.

During his periods of freedom between 1904 and 1913, Stalin worked diligently for the revolutionary movement and slowly made his way to a respectable position of leadership within Russian Marxism or, more precisely, within the Bolshevik faction that emerged after the movement divided into two in 1903. The split that year in the Russian Social Democratic Workers' Party, founded in 1898, concerned the seemingly minor question of how to define a party member. Vladimir Lenin (Ulyanov), a rising star in the movement, had published a short book in 1902, *What Is to Be Done?*, in which he argued for a highly centralized, elitist, hierarchically organized party whose members would in effect be professional revolutionaries. Given the authoritarian regime in Russia, only such a party, he claimed, could be effective in mobilizing the proletariat. At the Second Party Congress in 1903 he put forth a proposal defining a party member as anyone who subscribed to the party's program, gave it material support, and took part in the work of one of its organizations. A number of other socialist leaders, most notably Iulii Martov and Pavel Axelrod, offered a broader definition of a party member. They argued that anyone who gave 'regular personal support [to the party] under the guidance of one of [the party's] organizations' should qualify as a member in good standing. The difference in wording seemed to be minor, but in fact it was quite significant as the opponents of Lenin believed that only their definition of party membership could assure the emergence of a movement that truly represented the wishes of the masses.

In the vote on this issue, Lenin won by the smallest of margins, twenty-eight to twenty-three, and then only because some delegates had already walked out of the Congress to demonstrate their disagreement with the majority on other issues: the Bund (the labor organization of Jews in Lithuania, Poland, and Russia) because the delegates voted against granting it autonomy, and two other delegates because the Congress called for closing their newspaper, *Rabochee delo*, which had voiced criticisms of Lenin's political views.

In a brilliant move, Lenin immediately referred to his supporters as the *Bolsheviks* (Majoritarians) and the opponents the *Mensheviks* (Minoritarians). Lenin thus claimed that his followers represented the predominant sentiment at the Congress, and his opponents were remarkably inept in accepting the designation of having been in a minority, which was not the case. Had seven delegates not left the Congress because of disagreements with the delegates on other issues, Lenin's views on party membership would not have received the support of a majority.

To the average workers, whose support the Marxists were trying to enlist, the differences at the Congress may have seemed superficial, but in fact it soon became evident that, although both factions subscribed to a revolutionary cause, they represented two incompatible approaches on how to bring about fundamental political and economic changes in Russia. The Mensheviks tended to adopt more moderate tactics than the Bolsheviks, and this difference determined the outlook of the two factions on a wide range of major issues. By 1917, their reunification into one Marxist party was not a realistic possibility.

As soon as Stalin learned of the dispute at the Socialist Congress, he sided unequivocally with Lenin and threw in his lot with the Bolsheviks. He had been impressed by Lenin's earlier writings and there is some evidence that the two men had corresponded as early as 1903. Although Stalin occasionally differed with Lenin on some minor issues, on all fundamental questions of doctrine and tactics he invariably sided with him. Even when he had reached the pinnacle of power in the Soviet Union, he never failed to laud Lenin and to insist that his own policies were consistent with those of the founder of Bolshevism. At the same time, Lenin came to value Stalin's support and did his best to promote him within the ranks of the Bolshevik party. Only shortly before his death in 1924 did Lenin express serious misgivings about Stalin's character, but by then it was too late for him to impede his subordinate's ascent to the highest position of power in the Soviet Union.

Interestingly, the first time Stalin met Lenin, he was not impressed. His reaction is noteworthy because as a young man of twenty-six he had already formed a conception of political leadership that provides insight into how he would behave if he ever reached a position of power. His recollection of that meeting is worth quoting:

I met Lenin for the first time in December 1905 at the Bolshevik Conference at Tammerfors, Finland. I expected to see the mountain eagle of our Party as a great man, not only politically but [also] physically, for I had formed for myself a picture of Lenin as a giant, a fine figure of a man. What was my disappointment when I saw the most ordinary looking individual, below middle height, distinguished from ordinary mortals by nothing, literally nothing. A great man is permitted to be generally late at meetings so that those present may be apprehensive at his non-arrival, and so that before the great man's appearance there may be cries of 'Hush – silence – he is coming.' This ceremony seemed to me useful for it creates respect. What was my disappointment to find that Lenin had arrived before the delegates and was carrying on the most ordinary conversation, with the most ordinary delegates in a corner.

Stalin's disappointment must have been tempered by a sense of relief, for he was physically even less imposing than Lenin.

The meeting between the two Bolsheviks took place at a turbulent time in Russia: the country was still in the throes of the Revolution of 1905, the first significant upheaval from below in the country's history. Lenin later referred to it as the 'dress rehearsal' for 1917, by which he meant that events in the period from January 1905 until mid-1907 made inevitable the far more radical Revolution of 1917, when the tsarist regime was overthrown, paving the way for the assumption of power by the Bolsheviks. Lenin's assessment of the significance of the Revolution of 1905 to 1907 is not convincing, for during the decade from 1907 to 1917 a series of events, most notably the outbreak of World War I, led to the collapse of tsarism and opened the door to a seizure of power by the Bolsheviks. Still, the turbulence during the years from 1905 to 1907 was momentous and should have served as a warning to the men in power.

LENIN'S ROAD TO BOLSHEVISM

Vladimir Ilych Ulyanov, alias Lenin, was born on 22 April 1870, into a well-to-do, well-educated family in Simbirsk, now named Ulyanovsk, a city on the Volga river about 890 kilometers from Moscow. His father, the grandson of serfs, became a teacher and eventually the director of 450 primary schools. His mother, the daughter of a Jewish doctor who had converted to Orthodox Christianity, was also highly educated.

Vladimir was deeply influenced by the fate of his older brother, Alexander (Sasha), who as a student at St. Petersburg University had joined a movement dedicated to achieving the abolition of absolutism by assassinating Tsar Alexander III. Sasha undertook to create a bomb for the attack, but the police got wind of the plan, and he was arrested, tried, and immediately executed (in May 1887) by hanging.

That year, Vladimir enrolled in Kazan University, where he joined a radical political movement. His brother's execution prompted him to announce that 'there is another way' to struggle against the autocracy: by organizing a mass movement. The police apprehended him and he was sentenced, without a trial, to three years of exile in eastern Siberia, where he so greatly admired the river Lena that he adopted the pseudonym 'Lenin'. He continued his studies for a law degree at home and at the same time studied Marxism, which he embraced. In 1902, he published *What Is to Be Done?*, in which he advocated the formation of a tightly knit party of professional revolutionaries; it became the blueprint for the organization of the Bolshevik party.

One reason for the outburst of hostility to the tsarist regime was the recent formation of political parties, in addition to the Marxist parties already mentioned, that helped inspire those who were disaffected to give vent to their anger. In 1901, a group of intellectuals formed the Party of Socialist Revolutionaries (SRs), who contended that since the peasants had already been exposed to egalitarian principles of the commune, an institution that regulated local affairs of the villagers, the country could attain socialism without passing through the stage of full-blown capitalism. In

1904, the liberals, representing middle-class citizens who favored a sharp curtailment of monarchical power and the adoption of the rule of law, formed an underground organization known as the Union of Liberation. In the fall and winter of 1904–5, this party unleashed an extensive campaign for constitutional change. Despite their differences, all these parties played an active role in agitating for fundamental political changes.

If one defines a revolution in traditional Marxist terms as an upheaval during which power passes from one social class to another, the events during the two years from 1905 to mid-1907 do not qualify as a revolution. On the other hand, the chaos of that period and the inability of the government to enforce its will were so marked that no other term seems satisfactory. The challenge to the established order came from mass movements representing four different social groups: liberals among the middle class and gentry, industrial workers, peasants, and some of the national minorities. Serious disturbances broke out in various cities, agrarian regions, and outlying areas of the Empire, as well as in many cultural institutions and in the army and navy. Virtually no social group or geographical region remained unaffected by unrest. The government was able to survive these disorders only because they did not occur simultaneously. But in some regions the onslaught against the authorities forced tsarist officials to flee, which left the responsibility for local government temporarily in the hands of the insurgents.

The currents of rebellion were so diverse that at times it seemed as though Russia was undergoing not one revolution but a whole series of parallel revolutions. Nevertheless, since the numerous disturbances were part of a larger pattern of protest against the old regime, we can speak of a single revolution.

The upheaval of 1905 was actually a new type of revolution, the first in which a Marxist movement made its mark on an agrarian society, and as such it foreshadowed in some important respects the convulsions that have taken place in developing countries in recent decades. True, the old order survived, but at times it hovered on the brink of collapse. More important, the Empire's political system had been changed in significant ways. Even though the Tsar still claimed to rule as an autocrat, the claim was not convincing as long as the Duma, an elected legislative body established during the Revolution of 1905, continued to exercise certain political functions, as it did till the end of the old regime. Neither the ruler nor the bureaucracy could operate as arbitrarily as they had before the revolution. That the Duma was a vibrant institution was demonstrated with special force during the crisis of the old regime in 1916 and 1917, when it sharply criticized the tsarist government and made the critical decisions on the locus of power after the abdication of Nicholas II.

Moreover, from 1907 until 1917 Russia lived under a multi-party system, also a legacy of the revolution. Despite the restrictions still imposed by the government, newspapers and journals could deal with sensitive political and social issues in a way that was unimaginable before the revolution. Finally, the trade union movement survived all the restrictions imposed upon it after the end of the revolution, and maintained a measure of influence among the working class that it had not had prior to the revolution.

By 1905, Stalin had risen to a fairly important position in the Bolshevik movement, although he did not play a major role on the national scene during the intense struggles between workers and the authorities. He spent most of his time in Georgia, where he vigorously expounded Lenin's ideas in a series of polemical articles, but that region of the Empire was not the ideal place for such activities because Menshevism predominated among Social Democratic activists there. Stalin's reputation in Bolshevik circles rose significantly after the revolution, when he succeeded handsomely in securing funds – illegally – for his party. Money was perennially in short supply within the Bolshevik faction, in part because Lenin, as noted, insisted on a party of professional revo- lutionaries, individuals who devoted all their time to working for the Bolshevik cause. These activists had to be supplied with funds for personal needs, and in addition the organization had to bear the cost of printing and distributing newspapers and leaflets to keep their followers informed of demonstrations and political developments in the Empire. The Bolsheviks came up with an effective and highly controversial scheme for raising funds, the so-called 'expropriations' or 'partisan actions', lofty terms for armed bank robberies.

It had been known ever since 1907 that Stalin had played an important role in these robberies, but until the collapse of the Soviet Union in 1991, when the Georgian archives were opened to scholars, the details were murky. According to the historian Montefiore, the archival documents revealed that Stalin 'master- minded the operation' at the State Bank in Tiflis, which took place on 13 June 1907, and was the most ambitious of all the robberies. Stalin laid the groundwork by 'groom[ing] ... inside men' in the bank for many months and then 'presided over the operation'. When the attack began, 'there were up to fifty gang- sters raining bombs from the roofs, if not from Holy Mountains,' onto the square where the bank was located. Several people in the street nearby were killed, but none of the 'gangsters were caught'. Amazingly, the bank's officers were not sure whether the robbers left with 250,000 or 341,000 rubles, but scholars estimate that their haul would be worth about $3.4 million today; the loot's purchasing power in 1907 was considerably higher.

Much of the money was sent to Lenin, who was so fasci- nated by the 'daredevil Koba' (Stalin's name at the time), that he now referred to him in a friendly spirit as the 'Caucasian bandit'. But the haul was not as valuable as the Bolsheviks had assumed. A large portion was in notes of five hundred rubles and since the Russian government had given their serial numbers to banks in Western Europe, quite a few Bolshevik agents were arrested when they tried to exchange them for other currencies. The Russian police seem not to have been aware of Stalin's role in the robbery; when they arrested him on 25 March 1908, they did so on different charges.

Within the Russian Social Democratic Party – both the Bolsheviks and the Mensheviks were still members of a single organization – the robberies created a scandal that embittered relations between the two factions. The Menshevik leader Martov was so appalled by the Tiflis affair that he argued that it was 'a very convenient basis for an honest split which would be fully understood by the public'. That did not happen then, but for several years the robberies continued to be a divisive issue in the relations between the Bolsheviks and Mensheviks. Even as late as the 1920s, when Stalin was maneuvering to succeed Lenin as leader of the country, his opponents brought up his criminal conduct as a young revolutionary. Yet it did not impede his climb to power.

Long before he began that climb, Lenin boosted Stalin's position in the Bolshevik movement. First, Lenin arranged his appointment in 1912 to the bureau that dealt with operations of the party throughout the country. Stalin was paid fifty rubles a month, just enough to cover his personal expenses. He traveled widely to organize workers and enlist them into the Bolshevik movement. A year later, Lenin encouraged him to complete a task he had already begun and promised to bring him to the attention of a wide circle of party members. Sensitive to the growing demands of ethnic minority groups within the Empire for autonomy and even for independence, Lenin considered it politically necessary for the Bolsheviks to formulate a position on that subject that would be widely acceptable to those groups. Lenin's position on the issue had not been clear-cut: on the one hand, he favored the right of self-determination by minorities even to the point of separation from the state, but on the other hand he hoped to persuade all workers regardless of their ethnicity to join a single organization in the struggle for socialism. Someone was wanted who could write a theoretical piece to clarify the party's position on this vexing issue, which could lead to splits within the Bolshevik movement.

It would be difficult to think of a more complicated and provocative issue in Russia in the early twentieth century than the national question, which had deep roots in the country's history. The Russian Empire was the accretion of centuries of colonization, military conquest, and annexation by Muscovite rulers of weak principalities, whose culture differed from that of the conqueror. The Great Russians, as the ethnic Russians were known, composed no more than about forty-five percent of the population, yet they exerted paramount influence in politics; they occupied most of the important positions in the bureaucracy and the military services.

Tsars Alexander III (1881–94) and Nicholas II (1894–1917) embarked on a policy of ruthless Russification, which is best defined as an attempt to assimilate non-Russian minorities by persuading or forcing them to abandon their culture and in particular their language in favor of the culture of the so-called Great Russians. The two Tsars adopted that policy in part for security reasons. Concentrated in the borderlands, the minorities were looked upon as a potential danger in time of war. In addition, the Tsars feared that the special rights and privileges, cultural as well as political, enjoyed by some of the nationalities (notably the Finns and, to a much lesser degree, the Poles) would serve as a model for other minorities, among whom national consciousness was beginning to take root. If autonomy were widely extended, the Empire would cease to be a 'unitary state', to use the parlance of the time, and the Tsar's power would be sharply curtailed.

But the Tsars and their subordinates were also deeply influenced by prejudice. They considered the minorities to be culturally inferior, and they were especially antagonistic toward the Jews, who numbered about five million and on whom the government imposed economic, legal and social restrictions that were far more extensive and demeaning than the measures taken against any other group. At bottom, the hostility toward Jews derived from the belief that they were marked by 'innate vices' that made their full assimilation into Russian society impossible. The prominence of Jews in radical movements and, to a lesser extent, in the liberal movement was in large measure the fruit of the government's discriminatory policies.

Stalin seemed to be the ideal person to undertake the task of formulating a position on the national issue for the Bolsheviks. He came from a humble background and had been brought up in a region dominated by an ethnic minority with its own language and culture, yet he himself was entirely comfortable, professionally and culturally, in a party dominated by people who considered themselves Russian. In fact, in his first publication on the national question in 1904 he had indicated in rather strong language that he had little sympathy for the national aspirations of minorities, including those of the Georgians. But the work he produced on the national issue in 1913 under the tutelage of Lenin was more nuanced and more sensitive to the wishes of the country's ethnic groups.

In the fall of 1912 he traveled to the Polish city of Cracow, then the residence of Lenin, and during his stay there he discussed the national question with the founder of Bolshevism, after which he completed a long essay entitled *Marxism and the National Question* that substantiated his aim to be recognized as a theorist of Marxism. In a simple, even simplistic and at times polemical, style, Stalin criticized the views of other left-wing writers on the subject, most notably the Austrian Otto Bauer, who favored 'national-cultural autonomy' for minorities and also advocated organizing the Socialist Party along national or autonomous lines. Stalin then offered his definition of a nation: 'A nation is a historically constituted, stable community of people formed on the basis of a common language, territory, economic life and psychological make-up manifested in a common culture.' Thus, Russia and the Austro-Hungarian Empire were national states 'consisting of several nationalities', but the Jews were not because they 'belong to different nations'. Eventually, all national movements would disappear but not before the 'downfall of the bourgeoisie'. In the meantime, the policy of Marxist revolutionaries should be to permit minorities to maintain their own culture: if the minorities were granted the right to use their native language, run their own schools, and enjoy religious liberty – Stalin called this 'regional autonomy' – they would no longer demand national independence.

Lenin, who strongly opposed autonomous organizations – such as the Bund – for different national groups committed to Marxism, was pleased with Stalin's work and now declared him to have risen to the status of a respectable interpreter of Marxism. Yet, as will become clear below, in 1917, when the Bolsheviks were desperate to win the support of the national minorities, Lenin advocated a more radical option for them, the right to secede. After gaining power, the Bolsheviks reverted to the policy advocated by them in 1913, the granting of cultural autonomy to minorities.

By this time, Stalin's personal life had also taken a new turn. Ever since his late teens he had had the reputation of being something of a ladies' man, but in 1902 or thereabouts he settled down and married Ekaterina Semyonovna Svadnidze, the daughter of a railway employee, who was active in the Social Democratic Party. Data on the relationship between Stalin and Ekaterina is sparse. It is known that in 1906, when a baby was on the way, a formal church ceremony took place. Ekaterina was not an intellectual and, unlike Stalin, was not hostile to religion; in fact, she was devout and wanted her husband to return to the fold, pure wishful thinking on her part. Nevertheless, she was devoted to him. In 1907, she gave birth to a son, Yakov; a year later she contracted a serious illness and died. The infant was then placed in the care of his aunt, Ekaterina's sister. Stalin showed no interest in the boy and the relationship between father and son became troubled. At the age of twenty or twenty-one Yakov was deeply depressed, in large measure because of his father's mistreatment, and in a moment of despair tried to commit suicide by shooting himself. He incurred an injury but survived, which led Stalin to make the following insensitive remark: 'Ha! He couldn't even shoot straight.'

STALIN AND SON YAKOV

Stalin's two wives gave birth to three children – two sons and a daughter – and his relations with all of them were complicated and strained. But his attitude toward his first-born, Yakov, was so hostile that it deserves special attention. Stalin's first wife, Ekaterina Svanidze, gave birth to Yakov in 1907. When she died of typhus soon after, Stalin was devastated by this loss but was so dedicated to his revolutionary activities that he refused to care for his son; Yakov was sent to live with his grandmother and aunt in Tiflis, Georgia, where he was raised for thirteen years. Apparently, he only moved back to Moscow because his uncle, Alexander Svadnidze, advised him to in order to prepare for university studies. Once he returned to his own family, his first task was to learn Russian – his language for thirteen years had been Georgian.

Yakov got along with Stalin's other two children, Svetlana and Vasily, but his father could not stand him. Stalin belittled him, referring to him as a 'mere cobbler' and 'my fool'. After completing high school Yakov announced that he did not want to go to university and also let it be known that he planned to marry a sixteen-year-old girl he had met at school. Stalin would not hear of it. Yakov was so distressed that he put a pistol to his head and fired, but only wounded himself. According to the historian Stephen Kotkin, Stalin, in a letter to his second wife, dismissed his son as a 'hooligan and blackmailer, who does not have and never could have anything more to do with me'.

3

Stalin under Lenin's Leadership, 1917–1924

In January 1917, Lenin, then in Zurich, delivered a lecture to young workers in which he predicted that his listeners were likely to be so fortunate as to witness the 'coming proletarian revolution', but he doubted whether he would have the opportunity to participate in that event: 'We of the older generation may not live to see the decisive battles of this coming revolution.' Even so astute an analyst of social and political developments as Lenin did not grasp the significance of the impact on Russian society of the world war that had broken out in August 1914. But nor did anyone else. Most socialist leaders in Russia thought that it would take another twenty to thirty years before the proletariat would be in a position to stage a socialist revolution.

It is now generally acknowledged that no responsible leader in Europe planned or wanted a conflagration that would embroil much of the continent as well as the United States of America, Turkey, and eight other countries far from Europe. In July and August of 1914 statesmen all over Europe made one miscalculation after another and literally stumbled into a war that cost millions of lives, fundamentally changed the political order in several European countries, and in many ways influenced the course of world history. To give but two examples, it is highly unlikely that, without the destruction and pain in human suffering caused by the military conflict, either Hitler or the Bolsheviks would have reached the heights of power in Germany and Russia.

The immediate cause of the crisis that led to World War I was an assassination on 28 June 1914 in Sarajevo, the capital of Bosnia, a region that was part of the Austro-Hungarian Empire. A Serbian nationalist had persuaded himself that the killing of Archduke Ferdinand, the heir to the throne of that empire, would result in the granting of independence to Bosnia, which would then join Serbia in the creation of a new Slavic state, Yugoslavia. But the government in Vienna feared that giving up Bosnia would unravel the Empire, which included other Slavs who would also demand independence. The Austro-Hungarian leaders appealed for help to the German government, which promised what amounted to unconditional support by giving Vienna the freedom to send an ultimatum to Serbia so harsh that it was bound to be rejected. When that happened, Austria-Hungary declared war on Serbia (on 28 July).

In the meantime, the tsarist government had warned that it would come to the aid of fellow Slavs. At the last minute, Kaiser Wilhelm II of Germany appealed to Nicholas not to take an irrevocable action, prompting the Tsar to rescind an order for a general mobilization and to replace it with partial mobilization intended as a warning to Austria-Hungary. But his senior military officials informed Nicholas that the general staff had no plans for limited mobilization and urged him to stick to his original order. The Tsar, clearly ill-informed on military matters, agreed, whereupon Germany followed suit by mobilizing its forces as a gesture of support for Austria-Hungary. Other Western powers hesitated for a while, but on 4 August Great Britain announced its support for Russia, which already had France on its side; all three powers feared that if they remained neutral, Germany would become the dominant power on the continent. Hostilities began that day, triggering a conflagration with consequences no one had expected and no government wanted.

For Russia, the war turned out to be an unmitigated disaster. At first, many citizens, in a burst of patriotism, supported the war effort. Some early victories of Russian forces in Prussia and Galicia seemed to justify the tsarist government's policies. But the tide turned quickly, and the Tsar's forces suffered one defeat after another. It soon became clear that the army was in many respects unprepared to fight the well-disciplined and effectively commanded German army. Most of the senior officers in the tsarist army were more concerned with advancing their own reputations than with creating an effective fighting force, and as a consequence they often made decisions without consulting fellow officers. And many ordinary soldiers were illiterate and had no understanding of why they were being sent into battle. Ignoring all these flaws, the leaders of the government were convinced that so long as the army was large enough it would be a formidable military force. Within one year the military grew to 9.7 million men, but it soon became clear that there were not enough competent officers and non-commissioned officers to train so large a force. Worse still, there was neither enough equipment nor food for the troops, who at times went into battle even without guns. On those occasions, only the men in the front lines carried firearms and when some of them fell in battle the men in the rear picked up the weapons of their dead comrades. Demoralization was widespread and increasingly Russian soldiers surrendered to the enemy without putting up a fight. By late 1915, the Germans had scored one victory after another and had penetrated deep into the Russian Empire.

On the home front, enthusiasm for the war declined as economic conditions deteriorated at an alarming pace. To make matters worse, the railway system, never very efficient, broke down, creating difficulties for the movement of supplies. Moreover, the military losses were staggering; by the time hostilities ended early in 1918, 650,000 men had lost their lives, over 2.5 million were wounded, and more than 3.5 million were prisoners of war or missing. The Tsar had no idea how to deal with the country's problems. His wife, whose influence at the Court in St. Petersburg was rising, urged him to cope with the crises by becoming 'more autocratic', advice that was irrelevant, especially since the Duma grew increasingly outspoken in criticizing and defying the political authorities. Early in 1917 the country stood on the brink of disaster.

In the initial period of the war, workers rarely went on strike, but as the cost of the conflict soared, strikes increased significantly. In 1915, about 550,000 workers left their jobs. Within two years, the number had risen markedly as living standards continued to decline, in good measure because of frequent food shortages; even bread, the staple for lower-class people, was in short supply. The government's attempt to prevent strikes by drafting workers of military age and sending them to the front or forcing them to work in factories as soldiers only increased the bitterness of the angry young men.

On 8 March 1917, International Women's Day, the revolution may be said to have begun, although no one knew that this day marked the start of an upheaval that would last at least eight months, and, if one includes the Civil War, the struggle may be said to have lasted three years. That day thousands of women in Petrograd (formerly St. Petersburg) joined strikers from the large Putilov factory who were demonstrating against the government with banners featuring the political slogan 'Down with the Autocracy'. The women urged other workers in metalworking factories to join the protesters. The police easily broke up this assemblage, but a day later about 200,000 demonstrators appeared on the streets. The day after that the crowds were even larger and, ominously, the Cossacks and then regular soldiers refused to use force to disperse them. More ominously still, on 12 March one regiment after another openly supported the demonstrators. Meanwhile the unrest had spread to other cities and political leaders began to pressure the Tsar to abdicate, which he reluctantly did on 15 March. A dynasty that had ruled Russia for three hundred years and had claimed to rule by divine right collapsed, to be replaced by a provisional government that promised to hold democratic elections to determine the political future of the country.

But it quickly became clear that the new authorities would face a political rival, creating enormous difficulties for the government, which desperately needed wide public support. In St. Petersburg and soon in many other localities, workers and soldiers voted for the establishment of soviets (councils), which initially were dominated by Mensheviks and Socialist Revolutionaries. Within weeks, the Bolsheviks began to gain representation in the soviets, which became increasingly powerful and called for measures far more radical than those of the Provisional Government. And if the government could not count on the support of the soviets, it would not be able to enforce its will. Consequently, a system of 'dual power' developed, which meant that the government could not exercise political power by itself, but the soviets, the repository of considerable mass support, refused to assume any responsibilities of government and, more important, refused to support the decisions of the authorities. As a result, the Russian Empire was in effect rudderless at a time of war, when the country faced daunting military, economic, and social problems.

When unrest erupted in St. Petersburg, Stalin was still in exile in the Turukhansk region of Yenisei Province in the Arctic Circle, a place so isolated from the rest of the Russian Empire that escape was virtually impossible. Most of the time during this period of exile, Stalin avoided contact with people, even with other revolutionaries, who considered him haughty. But he did occasionally meet one fellow exile, Yakov M. Sverdlov, who already was known as an up-and-coming activist, in large part because of his administrative talents. Sverdlov was so highly regarded in Bolshevik party circles that in 1917 he was appointed head of state with the title of Chairman of the Central Executive Committee of the

All-Russian Congress of Soviets, and he remained in that position until his premature death at the age of thirty-three in March 1919. In 1914, Sverdlov offered a brief, not exactly favorable, assessment of Stalin, whom he described as a 'good fellow, but too much of an individualist in everyday life'. Stalin preferred reading books to cultivating friendships with other prisoners.

One of the first decisions of the Provisional Government was to set political prisoners free, and Stalin wasted no time in beginning the long trek west. In late March 1917, he arrived in Petrograd, where he immediately became active in political work by joining the editorial board of *Pravda*, the main publication of the Bolsheviks. Interestingly, he and L. B. Kamenev, the other notable Bolshevik then in the capital, adopted a moderate position on the war by supporting the government's policy of continuing the fight against Germany and Austria, although they also called on their followers to exert pressure on the government to seek an end to the conflict. In addition, they wanted to establish contact with the Mensheviks, in the hope of reaching an agreement to unify the two Marxist factions. Still committed to the traditional Marxist view that the bourgeois revolution must be completed before the second, socialist revolution could be attempted, Stalin did not believe that the time was ripe for an assault on the new government.

All this changed soon after Lenin's arrival in Petrograd on 16 April. He immediately issued the April Theses, which called for a radical stance vis-à-vis the Provisional Government. Although Lenin had declared a few weeks earlier in Zurich that a proletarian revolution was unlikely to break out in the near future, he now sensed that his timetable had been faulty. It was Lenin's genius to recognize in the early stage of the upheaval in Russia that the men who had replaced the tsarist officials would be too weak to govern effectively because large sectors of the population were deeply disaffected and demanded radical changes far beyond those envisioned by the new prime minister, Prince

Gyorgy Lvov. In the April Theses Lenin urged his followers not to compromise with the Provisional Government and to wage a relentless campaign against the war, including the encouragement of soldiers at the front to cease fighting and to fraternize with the enemy. In addition, he called for a drive to persuade the masses to support a seizure of power by the soviets.

Lenin's Bolshevik colleagues were taken aback by their leader's proposals, which they considered totally unrealistic. At one meeting where Lenin gave a speech advocating his strategy, the audience simply laughed. No other socialist supported Lenin's radical program, but this did not deter him. The unchallenged leader of Bolshevism from the time of the movement's founding, Lenin was not easily shaken in his beliefs, and the power of his authority in the Bolshevik movement was such that resistance to his proposals crumbled quickly. Within days of Lenin's arrival in Petrograd, Stalin abandoned his views on Bolshevik tactics and fervently subscribed to Lenin's proposals.

Over the next few months, conditions in the Russian Empire continued to deteriorate rapidly, making Lenin's policies increasingly plausible. In the military conflict with Germany and Austria, the performance of the Russian Army was disastrous; the peasants, who had long believed that they had insufficient land, seized the holdings of landlords, and no one could stop them; in urban areas, workers seized factories after expelling owners and managers; throughout the country, soviets seized control of local institutions of government; and national minorities in many parts of the Empire took matters into their own hands and declared their autonomy or independence. About two million soldiers, eager to take part in the land seizures, deserted and returned to their homes. The Provisional Government pleaded with the people not to support these mass movements, but few paid attention. Lenin's strategy proved to be sound and in following his advice, the Bolsheviks bolstered their influence among the populace, increasing the likelihood of widespread support for an overthrow of the authorities in Petrograd.

Early in September 1917, ardent defenders of the old regime under the leadership of General Lavr Kornilov organized an attempt to seize power so as to prevent the left from overthrowing the government. It was in many ways a bizarre and bungled effort that was easily defeated, but the consequences for the Provisional Government were devastating. Support for the Bolsheviks rose immensely, prompting Lenin to persuade his colleagues to launch an uprising against the government on 7 November. The misgivings of some leading Bolsheviks about the advisability and feasibility of seizing power proved to be without merit; as Lenin noted early in 1918, bringing down the government was 'extremely easy'. By late 1917, several observers noted, power lay in the street waiting to be picked up. The Bolshevik party, with a membership of about two hundred thousand, took power in the name of the proletariat, which numbered perhaps 3.5 million out of a population of 150 million.

Stalin was not a leader of the first rank in the dramatic events that led to the Bolshevik seizure of power in 1917. He did not come up with any new ideas to arouse working-class support for Bolshevism, nor did he play a significant role in organizing the workers for an assault on the government. Part of the reason for his secondary role is that he was not a fiery orator who could rouse the masses, a skill much valued and needed during the tense months of 1917. All in all, he was far less important than Leon Trotsky, who planned the strategy for the seizure of power and remained physically and politically close to Lenin during the hours when the Bolsheviks made their move against the Provisional Government. This difference in the roles of Trotsky and Stalin in 1917 helps to explain the fierce rivalry that emerged between the two men in the 1920s, which was a critical factor in the history of the Soviet Union.

But it would be a mistake to dismiss Stalin's work in 1917 as unimportant; he was Lenin's loyal subordinate and he efficiently handled numerous chores considered essential in advancing the cause of Bolshevism. It is no exaggeration to refer to Stalin as Lenin's right-hand man, his 'chief of staff'. That Lenin valued his competence and loyalty became clear when the new government was announced.

Stalin was appointed 'People's Commissar for Nationality Affairs', an important position in a country where, the Bolsheviks rightly believed, over a hundred ethnic groups had to be won over for the new regime to retain power. Of course, Stalin's publication on the nationality question, discussed above, seemed to make him the ideal person for this post. Furthermore, he was known to be a good organizer and the department had to be created from scratch since no such institution had existed in tsarist days. At first, Stalin's office consisted of one room in the Smolny Institute and he was granted a modest budget of three thousand rubles. Only after the government moved to Moscow in March 1918 was Stalin assigned an office – in the Kremlin – that was appropriate for someone who occupied a position considered necessary for the consolidation of power.

Perhaps more indicative of Stalin's rise to eminence was his appointment to the Politburo, which included four of the most prominent party leaders, Lenin, Trotsky, L. Kamenev, and Nikolai I. Bukharin, and which in effect served as the national government on a day-to-day basis. Stalin took on the task of running the everyday affairs of the party. According to the historian Isaac Deutscher, who was not enamored of Stalin, 'Like none of his colleagues, he was immersed in the party's daily drudgery and all its kitchen cabals.' Within a few years, as we shall see, the members of the Politburo would come to realize that they had made a mistake in giving Stalin a free hand in administering affairs that seemed trivial but in effect were politically of great importance.

John Reed, an American journalist who went to Petrograd in 1917 to report on the progress of the revolution, was one of the first to recognize Stalin's political gifts. Shortly before his death in 1920, Reed wrote that Stalin 'is not an intellectual like the other people you will meet. He's not even particularly well informed, but he knows what he wants. He's got will-power, and he's going to be on top of the pile some day.' It was a remarkable insight because in the first years after the revolution Stalin never revealed his ambitions and it is not clear that in the early years of Bolshevik rule he himself thought of reaching the pinnacle of power. Lenin, after all, was relatively young – forty-seven at the time of the Bolshevik Revolution – and he gave no sign of serious illness. Stalin was content to adopt a stance that made him indispensable to Lenin. He never turned down an assignment and efficiently carried out those tasks that were considered too menial and uninteresting by his colleagues in the Politburo, who preferred to work on problems that they believed required deep knowledge of Marxist philosophy.

Interestingly, Kamenev, Grigory Zinoviev, and to some extent Trotsky, three prominent Bolsheviks who within a few years became Stalin's enemies, favored his appointment to the various senior posts. All three believed that Stalin was the right person for what they regarded as unexciting positions. But in fact conditions in Russia were so chaotic that the government had to focus on practical issues such as ending the war, strengthening its hold on power, dealing with foreign military intervention largely designed to aid groups bent on overthrowing the regime, improving the economy, and assuring the ethnic minorities that their special needs would be dealt with sympathetically. The three sponsors of Stalin were correct in believing that he was the right person to be in charge of solving practical problems. They could not foresee that his success in that work would prove to be a great asset in the political struggles that dominated the 1920s. Notably, once Stalin was the undisputed leader, he had all three killed.

Lenin's first concern was to end the war with Germany. The Russian army demonstrated little resolve to resist the enemy, and by November 1917 German troops occupied vast stretches of the Empire. Lenin knew that continuing the conflict would undermine the Bolshevik hold on power. 'We must sign the terms set down [by the German government],' he declared. 'If you do not sign, you sign the death sentence of the Soviet power in three weeks.' He was willing to accept a treaty that would give Germany control over the Baltic provinces, Belorussia, and the Ukraine even though that would deprive the country of a sizable portion of its population as well as considerable industrial and agricultural resources. Left-wing Bolsheviks led by Bukharin and Trotsky were convinced that the revolution would soon spread to Central Europe and that there was therefore no need to accept such harsh conditions, and they convinced enough other Bolshevik leaders to vote against Lenin's proposal to succeed in defeating it. When it became clear to German leaders that Russia was not ready to capitulate, they ordered their forces to penetrate further into its territory. At that point, in March 1918, Lenin managed to secure support for his position, and the Bolsheviks signed a peace treaty in Brest-Litovsk that made extensive concessions to Germany. Lenin's analysis proved to have been sound. Russia could now focus on domestic issues and, moreover, after Germany's defeat later in 1918, Russia regained most of the lands it had surrendered.

Lenin's second task was to defeat two attempts to crush the revolution. The French, British, American and Japanese governments sent troops into Russia to undermine the new government, but their efforts were half-hearted and ended early in 1921. Much more serious was the attempt by the so-called White armies, led by former officers of the tsarist army, to overthrow the Bolshevik government. This conflict, known as the Civil War, lasted over two years, from late 1918 to early 1921, and proved to be enormously costly in human lives. It has been suggested that the bitterness engendered by the Civil War helps explain the increasing radicalism of the Bolsheviks.

Lenin appointed Trotsky as Commissar for War, confident that he would discharge his duties efficiently. It soon became clear that Trotsky had little patience for subordinates he considered incompetent or who disagreed with him on how to conduct the war. One such subordinate was Stalin, and from the beginning of the Civil War, the two men differed fundamentally over how to organize the government's forces. When filling important positions in the Red Army, Trotsky favored appointing men who had served in the tsarist army but now supported the revolution. He insisted that their skills in warfare were needed to build up an effective force. Stalin rejected this approach on the ground that these officers could not be trusted.

Early in June 1918, Stalin was sent to Tsaritsyn, on the western bank of the Volga river, to collect much-needed grain, but he soon became involved in military matters. The war against the counterrevolutionaries was not going well in the area even though the Bolsheviks enjoyed a clear-cut superiority in forces. On 19 July, Stalin was appointed head of the local revolutionary council, the highest local authority on military issues. He remained in charge for several months, but conditions continued to deteriorate militarily. According to Trotsky, Stalin disregarded his orders, and 'every day I would receive from the high command or the front commands such complaints against Tsaritsyn as: it is impossible to get executions of an order, it is impossible to find out what is going on there, it is even impossible to get an answer to an inquiry.' On 10 January 1919, he wrote to Lenin that 'I consider Stalin's patronage of the Tsaritsyn policy a most dangerous ulcer, worse than any treason or betrayal by military specialists.'

During the months that Stalin refused to listen to Moscow he revealed traits that would be widely recognized only after he became the leader of the country in 1929. He resented orders from others (Lenin was the exception) and, convinced that he was more capable than anyone else – even in military strategy – he made his own decisions on many vital issues. Occasionally, he went so far as to write 'To be ignored' on orders Trotsky had sent to the military commander in the south, General Kliment Voroshilov, who was under Stalin's command. Trotsky was so frustrated that he finally sent a cable to Lenin demanding action: 'I insist categorically on Stalin's recall.' Lenin had wanted to avoid such drastic action because he knew that Stalin would resent it, but in the end he followed Trotsky's advice. Stalin never forgot the slight.

By early 1920, the Bolsheviks had defeated the Whites and most of the foreign interventionist troops had left the country. But the Bolsheviks still faced enormous economic and political problems. In the cities, there was a real danger of starvation because of a severe shortage of grain, a consequence of the unwillingness of peasants to sell their produce at the prevailing very low prices. Industrial production had declined by more than two thirds, leaving many workers unemployed. Moreover, the transportation system had deteriorated to such an extent that in some regions of the country products that were available could not be shipped to markets.

The government attempted to deal with these problems by introducing socialism under the rubric of War Communism, but this effort failed miserably. The central feature of the economic program was the creation of a state monopoly on grain. On the government's initiative, poor peasants formed village committees to requisition grain from well-off peasants, by force if necessary. As an incentive to the committees, their members were promised a share of the grain they seized as well as a share of the industrial goods available for the villages. Thus were the ideological underpinnings of War Communism laid bare: it brought class warfare, often accompanied by ghastly outbursts of violence, into the countryside.

In November 1918, the government nationalized trade and established a network of state cooperative stores authorized to distribute goods. Because of the pervasive shortages, a system of rationing was introduced. Two months later, the government nationalized all banks and began to print money at a feverish pace to pay for its expenditures. The predictable result was rapid inflation, which prompted the authorities to replace the system of monetary taxation with taxation in goods. Workers' control of factories, which had been approved in September 1917, remained in force, even though industrial production declined at an alarming rate, by 1920 to about thirteen percent of the 1913 level. Meanwhile, by the second half of 1918 about twenty-eight percent of all wages were paid in kind and in three years this figure rose to ninety-four percent. In effect, Russia had been transformed into a barter economy, which continued to worsen because the peasants, rather than turn their crops over to the committees of the poor, decided to reduce output.

Within four years of the revolution, agricultural production declined to fifty-four percent of the 1913 level. It has been estimated that in the years from 1918 to 1920 over seven million people died of malnutrition. Many citizens living in cities returned to the countryside; Moscow and St. Petersburg, to cite but two examples, lost about half their population. But the Bolsheviks could claim some positive results from War Communism: they secured control over the so-called commanding heights of the economy, that is, over heavy industry, transportation, banks, and foreign trade. And they gained some administrative experience, which would serve them well in the future.

Nevertheless, Lenin realized that the price the Russian people had to pay for this achievement was much too high and that if conditions did not improve the new system could be endangered. There were, in fact, signs that increasing numbers of people were becoming restless. Peasant uprisings, which had increased at an alarming rate in the fall of 1920, became so intense in Tambov that it took the government four years to quash them.

In 1921, Lenin decided to change course. He adopted what came to be known as the New Economic Policy, which marked a measured return to capitalism. The government abolished compulsory requisitioning of agricultural products, peasants were allowed to sell most of their products on the free market, and a bank was established that did business along traditional lines. In addition, individuals could now own small factories, although the government retained control of larger enterprises that together employed about eighty-four percent of the labor force. Although the economic recovery was not always smooth, by 1928 the output of many branches of industry equaled that of 1913. Agricultural production also rose markedly, and by 1928 the standard of living of most people had returned more or less to the pre-war level. And if various 'socialized wages' such as health benefits, state insurance schemes and educational scholarships are taken into account, urban workers were better off in 1928 than they had been in 1913.

In the political arena, Lenin called for strengthening controls from above. Despite the great authority he had exercised ever since the Bolsheviks took power, he was not a dictator who simply issued orders that citizens had to obey. He permitted discussion of issues and differences of opinion within the communist movement. At times lively controversies characterized discussions at the highest party levels; decisions were reached by vote – and Lenin did not always have his way. But now that he had embarked on a program of economic reform he believed that the time had come to 'put a lid' on all opposition to his program. It was pointless, he contended, to reproach him for placing such limits on free speech, for it followed from the 'state of affairs', by which he presumably meant that the Bolsheviks were politically too weak to allow freedom of speech.

These were not the government's only efforts to stifle opposition. As early as December 1917, only weeks after the Bolsheviks seized power, the authorities had established the *Cheka*, or security police, charged with protecting the revolution, if necessary by shooting recalcitrant opponents of the government without regard to legal procedures. In response to criticism by party members of the actions by the police, Lenin scolded them as 'narrow-minded intellectuals' who 'sob and fuss' over the Cheka's 'mistakes'. During the first six months of its existence, the security police executed 882 people.

In the meantime, Stalin had become increasingly powerful among the political elite that ran the country. In 1922, Lenin arranged to have him appointed as General Secretary of the Communist Party, a position in which he would deal primarily with administrative matters such as planning of various Communist Party meetings, assigning work to party functionaries, and responding to the requests of ethnic minorities. The other Bolshevik dignitaries, who had a deep knowledge of Marxist theory, considered such work unsuitable and even inappropriate for them. They preferred to focus on work they considered more challenging and more important, namely, steering the country on a course that would lead to the realization of the ultimate goals of Marxism. But Stalin had a better understanding than his colleagues of how to advance in the world of politics. A few years after Lenin's death in 1924, the party member who occupied the post of General Secretary became by far the most powerful person in the country. Stalin never gave up the title and in every country that adopted the communist system after 1945 the leader held the title of General Secretary.

When the post was created, Lenin had in mind the leadership of a new department in charge of such administrative matters as the appointment and promotion of party functionaries. It did not take Stalin long to realize that people indebted to him for their positions in the Communist Party – soon quite lucrative and prestigious – would be grateful and most likely to support him if he was entangled in struggles for influence in the party.

As Commissar of Nationalities, the post to which he had been appointed in 1917, he could already count on the support of many party members among the national minorities, a large proportion of Russia's total population. Many of them were economically among the most disadvantaged people in the country and needed all the help they could get from the authorities in Moscow. Stalin went out of his way to listen sympathetically to their complaints and requests for help, and he often found ways to oblige. But he was shrewd enough not to reveal any personal ambition or to ask his supplicants for any favors. In a political movement that derided the importance of individuals in influencing the march of history, Stalin seemed to be an ideal leader. He appeared to be content to serve the people without expecting any rewards in return. It was a shrewd stance.

Stalin could be rude and nasty, but in the years before he became dictator of the Soviet Union (the name adopted in December 1922), he generally managed to control his temper. His most egregious lapse occurred on 21 December 1922, five days after Lenin suffered his second stroke. The first stroke, in March of that year, had weakened the Bolshevik leader, but he seemed to be recovering when he was afflicted again. Doctors had advised Nadezhda Krupskaya, Lenin's wife, that Lenin should be allowed to dictate letters for no longer than ten minutes a day, that he should not have any visitors, and that no attempt should be made to keep him abreast of current events. The Central Committee charged Stalin with enforcing these restrictions, and when he learned that with the permission of Professor Voerster, a medical consultant from Germany, Krupskaya had written a short letter to Trotsky that Lenin had dictated to her, he was furious. He called Krupskaya on the phone, and berated her in offensive language for having violated the orders of Lenin's regular doctors; he threatened to bring charges against her before the Central Control Commission, which had the authority to punish people who violated party discipline.

Krupskaya considered Stalin's call insulting, and in a letter to Kamenev dated 23 December she denounced Stalin for his 'most rude outburst against me'. She appealed to Kamenev, a member of the Central Committee, to 'protect me from rude interference in my personal life, unworthy abuse, and threats'. She was sure that the Control Commission would exonerate her, but 'I have no time or energy to spend on this stupid squabble. I too am a living person and my nerves are strained to the utmost.'

Sometime after this incident, Lenin learned of Stalin's conversation with his wife and on 5 March 1923, he dictated a letter to the General Secretary that began as follows: 'You had the rudeness to call my wife to the telephone and berate her.' He then told Stalin that although Krupskaya was prepared to forget the incident, he could not 'so easily forget what was done against my wife, and there is no need to point out that what is done to my wife I consider to be against me also. Therefore I ask you to consider whether you agree to take back what you said and apologize, or whether you prefer to break relations between us.' Stalin decided to apologize to Krupskaya, but it soon became known that Lenin had harbored serious misgivings about Stalin's character and fitness for a high position even before the outburst.

A month before that incident, Lenin, aware of the seriousness of his illness, had dictated a testament in which he evaluated the strengths and weaknesses of his leading subordinates and also touched on the escalating rivalry between Stalin and Trotsky. He noted that Stalin as General Secretary had amassed 'boundless power in his hands' and was 'not sure that he will always manage to use his power with sufficient caution'. Lenin considered Trotsky to be 'perhaps the most able man in the present C.C. [Central Committee]', but he also mentioned two of his drawbacks: 'his too far-reaching self-confidence and excessive absorption in the purely administrative side of things'. Lenin feared that the fierce rivalry between these two 'outstanding leaders of the C.C.' could lead to a split in the party if steps were not taken 'to prevent it'.

On 4 January 1923, he added a postscript that focused solely on Stalin's character and criticized him more pointedly than ever before. Lenin warned that he was so rude that his conduct, 'tolerable in our midst … becomes intolerable in the office of general secretary'. He therefore proposed the dismissal of Stalin from this office and the appointment of someone else 'who in all other respects falls on the other side of the scale from Comrade Stalin, namely, more tolerant, more loyal, more polite and more considerate of comrades, less capricious, etc.' At about the same time as he composed the testament, Lenin also published an article in *Pravda* criticizing Stalin as a poor administrator and again accusing him of rudeness, but the language of the article was so vague that it did not have a strong impact on party leaders.

Although Lenin's testament included acute insights into the characters of Stalin and Trotsky, the decision of a small group of party leaders not to make it public greatly reduced its political significance. It became a subject of discussion in the highest party circles only when a full year had elapsed since Lenin's death, which had occurred on 21 January 1924. He had never fully recovered from his first two strokes. For almost a year, he had been unable to speak, and during that period Stalin and Trotsky maintained a certain degree of restraint in battling each other. The two men retained this posture for about a year, a period during which the Communist Party remained rudderless. Then they began to vent their true feelings about each other and their aspirations became more evident.

Several days before the Thirteenth Party Congress was to meet (in May 1924), Krupskaya attempted to weaken Stalin politically by sending Kamenev a copy of Lenin's testament. She claimed that Lenin had requested that the testament be shown to the next Party Congress 'for its information'. Stalin, who could not automatically expect a majority at the Congress to support his wish to keep the testament secret, immediately turned to Zinoviev and Kamenev, who were persuaded to do Stalin's bidding. They were motivated by the conviction that Trotsky was a greater threat than Stalin to their own political ambitions. In keeping with their wishes, the Central Committee voted not to have the testament read to the Congress and to make it public only at closed meetings of selected groups of delegates, who would be told to keep in mind that Lenin was seriously ill when he drafted the document. The Committee also agreed that Stalin had performed satisfactorily in his various positions of leadership. Nevertheless, Stalin offered to resign from his post as General Secretary, but the Committee members voted not to accept his offer. Even Trotsky did not object to Stalin's reelection. It was a fateful decision for Russia, the communist movement, and even for much of Europe.

LEON DAVIDOVICH TROTSKY, 1879–1940

In hindsight, anyone studying the careers of Trotsky and Stalin would conclude that these two revolutionaries were bound to clash and become mortal enemies. They were the same age, both of them joined the Marxist movement in their late teens, each one of them was fiercely ambitious, and by 1917 both revered the founder and unquestioned leader of Bolshevism, Lenin. But in their personalities, natural gifts, and achievements, they differed markedly. Stalin was very clever as a politician and schemer, and knew how to organize a loyal following and to retain its support, often by recourse to brutal methods. His publications tended to be uninspiring. Trotsky could also deal harshly with opponents, but his gifts as a theorist of Marxism, as an organizer of military forces, and as a public speaker were beyond Stalin's reach. Not surprisingly, Lenin on his deathbed pronounced Trotsky to be the ablest man in the Politburo, the highest political organ in the Soviet Union.

Trotsky's contributions to Russian Marxism and to the success of the Revolution of 1917 were outstanding. In 1905 he formulated the theory of Permanent Revolution, in which he argued that Russia could skip the bourgeois revolution and move directly to socialism once the autocracy had been overthrown, which is essentially the path the Bolsheviks sought to follow after seizing power in 1917. In 1918, when the Bolshevik government faced a military threat from counterrevolutionaries, it was Trotsky who organized the Red Army, which defeated the so-called Whites. During the Civil War (1918–20), Trotsky clashed sharply with Stalin, who proved to be a poor military leader. From that moment, the two men were bitter enemies.

When Lenin became seriously ill in 1922, Trotsky was the obvious successor. But Trotsky was not an effective politician. Within a few years, Stalin outwitted him by mobilizing a large following in the communist movement. In 1929, he treated Trotsky as an outlaw and forced him to leave the Soviet Union. For several years, Trotsky sought asylum in several countries, but leaders in nearly all of them considered him to be too dangerous. Finally, he settled in Mexico. Even though he was now a defeated man, far from the bastion of communism, Stalin still feared him and in 1940 he ordered his loyal supporters to dispose of him. One of them hacked Trotsky to death with an axe in a suburb of Mexico City.

Lenin's testament was too important and too titillating to be kept secret for long. A small number of Communist Party functionaries heard about it, but the general public was essentially kept in the dark. There were vague rumors that such a document existed, although its contents remained murky. But it did reach a wider audience in the West. Apparently, Krupskaya released a copy to a party leader who handed it to the American writer Max Eastman, then a strong supporter of the Soviet Union. In October 1926, Eastman published Lenin's testament in the *New York Times*, having already made it public in 1925 in his book *Since Lenin Died*. The impact of this revelation on supporters of communism in the West was not very far-reaching, and it aroused even less interest in the Soviet Union, in part because Trotsky, at the demand of the Politburo, issued a signed statement that 'all talk about a testament' was a malicious lie designed to distort Lenin's will and undermine the Communist Party. It was only one of a series of signs of Trotsky's weakness in political combat.

LENIN'S TESTAMENT, 4 JANUARY 1923

A year before his death, Lenin composed the following statement, which indicated that he had reached the conclusion that Stalin's wings needed to be clipped if a split within the Communist Party was to be avoided:

> I think that the fundamental factor in the matter of stability [of the party] ... is such that members of the Central Committee as Stalin and Trotsky [are in bitter conflict]. The relation between them constitutes, in my opinion, a big half of the danger of that split ... the avoidance of which might be promoted, in my opinion, by raising the number of members of the Central Committee to fifty or one hundred.
>
> Stalin, having become General Secretary, has accumulated enormous power in his hands and I am not sure that he always knows how to use that power with sufficient caution. On the other hand, Trotsky, as was proved by his struggle against the Central Committee in connection with the question of the People's Commissariat of Ways and Communication, is distinguished not only by exceptional abilities – personally he is surely the ablest man in the present Central Committee – but also by his too far-reaching self-confidence and disposition to be much attracted by the purely administrative side of affairs.
>
> *Postscript*: Stalin is too rude and this fault ... becomes insupportable in the office of General Secretary. Therefore, I propose to the comrades to find a way to remove Stalin from that position and appoint to it another who differs from Stalin in being more patient, more loyal, more polite, more attentive to comrades and less capricious ... [This] is not a trifle, or it is such a trifle as may acquire decisive significance.

Stalin had gone to great lengths to minimize the damage of Lenin's criticisms of his behavior. He helped arrange an elaborate funeral for the departed leader as well as his embalming, which some people likened to the honors bestowed on a pharaoh. The speeches in honor of Lenin depicted him as having 'known, seen, foreseen everything' and having 'said and predicted everything'. Stalin delivered a speech on the eve of the funeral so laudatory that some listeners considered it 'strange'. It seemed that in trying to deify the departed leader he was harking back to his days as a theology student. The speech deserves to be quoted at length because it reveals the lengths to which Stalin was prepared to go to ingratiate himself with the Russian people by demonstrating his unconditional devotion to Lenin. It also gave the impression that he had always been in the good graces of the man who fundamentally changed the course of Russian history. And Stalin more than suggested that if he succeeded Lenin as leader, he would faithfully follow in his path. It ran as follows:

'In leaving us, Comrade Lenin commanded us to hold high and to keep pure the great name of Member of the Party. We swear to thee, Comrade Lenin, to honor thy command.

'In leaving us, Comrade Lenin ordered us to conserve the unity of our Party as the apple of our eye. We swear to thee, Comrade Lenin, to honor thy command.

'In leaving us, Comrade Lenin ordered us to maintain and strengthen the dictatorship of the proletariat. We swear to thee, Comrade Lenin, to exert our full strength to honor thy command.

'In leaving us, Comrade Lenin ordered us to strengthen with all our might the union of workers and peasants. We swear to thee, Comrade Lenin, to honor thy command.

'In leaving us, Comrade Lenin ordered us to strengthen and enlarge the Union of the Republics. We swear to thee, Comrade Lenin, to honor thy command.

'In leaving us, Comrade Lenin enjoined on us fidelity to the Communist International. We swear to thee, Comrade Lenin, to devote our lives to the enlargement and strengthening of the union of the workers of the whole world, the Communist International.'

Lenin, in many respects a modest person, would never have approved of such glorification. To be sure, he held strong views on political issues, and he fought hard to impose his will on the party, but he did not expect blind obedience and he did not enjoy what he considered excessive praise.

Trotsky, it was widely noted, did not attend the funeral or any of the party meetings honoring Lenin. Trotsky had taken ill a few days before Lenin's death and had been advised by his doctors to spend time in a more hospitable climate. During his journey to the east – while stopping off in Tiflis – he received a telegram from Stalin with the news that Lenin had died. Stalin told him that the funeral would take place the following Saturday, noting that 'you can't be back in time, and so we advise you to continue your treatment.' Trotsky, however, later learned that the funeral was scheduled for Sunday and as he put it in his autobiography, 'I could easily have reached Moscow by then.' He believed that Stalin wanted other Bolshevik leaders and the people at large to think that he was indifferent to Lenin's death, and that it was Stalin's way of sowing doubt about the authenticity of Trotsky's commitment to Bolshevism.

4
The Struggle for Power, 1924–1928

Stalin made his first public moves to succeed Lenin as head of the Bolshevik party after the latter's death, but he had laid the groundwork for it in 1923, during the second phase of Lenin's illness, when it became increasingly clear that the party would soon have to choose a new leader. Stalin joined two fellow members of the Politburo, Kamenev and Zinoviev, to form an alliance soon known as the triumvirate (*troika*), whose existence was acknowledged by Stalin in April 1923. Its primary purpose was to isolate and weaken Trotsky, widely regarded as the second most capable leader of the party. Early in 1923, Stalin began to attack Trotsky at meetings of the Politburo for inordinately craving power and for being a defeatist and pessimist because he insisted that the Soviet Union needed the support of other countries to reach its final goal of socialism. Kamenev and Zinoviev joined forces with Stalin because they had their own ambitions and also feared that Trotsky would take Lenin's place. It did not occur to them that Stalin might be a viable candidate to succeed Lenin. They believed that he lacked the intellectual and personal attributes necessary for leadership of the Soviet Union.

Trotsky's response to the initial machinations of the troika remains a puzzle, as does his behavior throughout the struggle for power, which did not end until 1927 or 1928. In 1923, Trotsky was so prominent and esteemed in party circles that he might have put an end to Stalin's intrigues if he had openly committed himself to a full-throated campaign against the troika. It may be, as some historians have suggested, that he was not convinced of Lenin's imminent death and therefore considered it unseemly to campaign for the leadership post. The problem with this analysis is that even after Lenin's death, Trotsky waged a rather inconsistent and at times listless struggle against the troika. It is also possible that Trotsky was so half-hearted in seeking to replace Lenin because he was afraid that many people would vehemently oppose having a Jew in the top position in the country. Shortly after the Revolution of 1917, he had turned down Lenin's suggestion that he become Commissar of Home Security, the second-highest position in the government at that time, because he did not think that most ordinary Russians would tolerate a Jew's presence in that post.

Or perhaps Trotsky simply underestimated Stalin, whom he dismissed as the 'most eminent mediocrity in our party', a judgement that was far off the mark. It is also conceivable that despite all of Trotsky's indisputable gifts, he was not cut out for the kind of infighting necessary to fend off his opponents. Moreover, in 1923, as mentioned above, Stalin's misbehavior toward Krupskaya and Lenin's sharp criticisms of Stalin were not widely known, and those who had heard of them agreed to remain silent. Under the circumstances, Stalin could engage in his intrigues without fear that he would encounter resistance from comrades in the upper echelon of the party.

Occasionally, Trotsky struck back by raising questions about the overall direction of the Soviet Union. He warned that the country was becoming 'bureaucratized' and called for a discussion of national issues not only in the Central Committee, whose membership ranged from seventy to one hundred, but also in the Communist Party as a whole. He wanted the debate to take place in the entire communist movement because he knew he was stymied in the Politburo, where Stalin commanded a majority.

But Stalin and his supporters would not agree to any proposal by Trotsky. Stalin's hatred for Trotsky was even more deep-seated than Trotsky's for Stalin, in large part because he envied his rival for his charisma, a quality Stalin knew he lacked. He and his colleagues in the triumvirate responded to Trotsky's request by accusing him, as they had during earlier disputes, of 'malevolence, personal ambition, [and] neglect of duty'.

The struggle for power intensified and became public soon after Lenin was enshrined in a small building in the grounds of the Kremlin. The conflict degenerated into a smear campaign: men who had dedicated themselves to creating a new and just order in which decency and egalitarianism would be the ultimate goal, abandoned politeness and all sense of proportion. The troika concentrated on belittling Trotsky and on isolating him within the upper echelon of the Communist Party. The three men harped on the fact that, prior to 1917, Lenin and Trotsky had had some sharp differences over strategy and even over theoretical questions; a leaflet appeared, entitled *What Ilyich Wrote and Thought about Trotsky,* that repeated all the criticisms Lenin had made of Trotsky's views in the years from 1904 to 1917. But in leveling these charges, they ignored that in 1917 and subsequently the two colleagues rarely differed on fundamental issues. Lenin had been unstinting in his praise of Trotsky for having organized the seizure of power in 1917 and for having masterminded the military struggle that the Bolsheviks waged against the opposition from 1918 to 1920. In fact, after the seizure of power in 1917, Lenin heaped extraordinary praise on the man who had stood by his side during the most trying period of the revolution: 'There is not a better Bolshevik than Trotsky.'

The struggle for power quickly spread and the invective intensified. Party members accused each other of insincerity, dishonesty, and, most offensive of all, not being true believers in Leninism and Bolshevism. Supporters of the troika dubbed Trotsky a 'political Bonaparte', which suggested that if he succeeded Lenin he would be dictatorial and reckless like Napoleon I. They increasingly denounced him as the 'grave-digger' of the Bolshevik Revolution, a charge that Trotsky had earlier leveled at Stalin. The political battles became confusing because at times individuals brazenly switched sides and in the process accused former colleagues of disloyalty, opportunism, and recklessness. Even now, it is hard to understand how people outside the Soviet Union who followed politics in that country could maintain confidence in the integrity of anyone who might emerge victorious from these conflicts.

In the initial period of the struggle for power, Stalin cleverly concealed his ambitions and succeeded in deluding his two lead-ing supporters, Kamenev and Zinoviev, about his ultimate aim, which is strange because his tactics were obvious.

As General Secretary, Stalin controlled patronage, and he used that power to send many of Trotsky's leading supporters abroad on diplomatic missions, far from the political conflicts in the Soviet Union. Stalin also had the authority to appoint party members to desirable positions within the Soviet Union; he increasingly used that power to build a loyal following within the party.

At the Thirteenth Party Congress in May 1924, only four months after Lenin's death, Trotsky faced a barrage of denun-ciation. Zinoviev demanded that Trotsky publicly recant all his criticisms of the Politburo majority. Zinoviev also declared that 'It is now a thousand times more necessary than ever that the party should be monolithic.' A few months earlier, Zinoviev had proposed expelling Trotsky from the Communist Party and had even suggested arresting him, but Stalin at that time was not prepared to go that far. He played the part of a moderate by declaring that a leadership of the party without Trotsky was 'unthinkable'. In light of the new attacks at the Congress, Trotsky felt called upon to defend himself and to explain his past behav-ior. His fascinating and puzzling – even contradictory – statement reveals much about his deepest convictions and also provides insight into his conduct during the years after Lenin's death; at the same time, it sheds additional light on his failure to defeat Stalin in the four-year battle to succeed Lenin:

> Nothing could be simpler or easier, morally and politically, than to admit before one's own party that one had erred ... No great moral heroism is needed for that ... Comrades, none of us wishes to be or can be right against the party. In the last instance the party is always right, because it is *the only historic instrument which the working class possesses for the solution of its fundamental tasks*. I have said already that nothing would be easier than to say before the party that all these criticisms and all these declarations, warnings, and protests were mistaken from the beginning to the end. I cannot say so, however, because, comrades, I do not think so. I know that one ought not to be right against the party. One can be right only with the party and through the party because history has not created any other way for the realization of one's rightness. The English have the saying 'My country, right or wrong'. With much greater justification we can say: My party, right or wrong – wrong on certain partial, specific issues or at certain moments ... It would be ridiculous perhaps, almost indecent, to make any personal statements here, but I do hope that in case of need I shall not prove the meanest soldier on the meanest of Bolshevik barricades.

Even after this statement, Trotsky continued to do battle against Stalin, but it is no exaggeration to suggest that he did so with one hand tied behind his back.

Stalin benefited from the barrage of abuse leveled at Trotsky, but he knew that he needed to do more to establish himself as Lenin's successor. He had to demonstrate that he had mastered the intricacies of Marxist thought and, more important, that he could make an original contribution to that field. His short work on the nationality question was not considered a major effort, especially since it was widely known that Lenin had tutored him and helped him write that work. In March 1923, Stalin tried to establish himself as an original thinker by publishing an article on 'strategy and tactics', which focused on Lenin's views on the topic, but party members did not regard it as particularly original, and it did not bring him the acclaim he sought. Scholars now generally agree that in writing the work Stalin had plagiarized from 'Lenin's Doctrine on Revolution' by Filipp Ksenofontov.

Late in 1924, Stalin made another attempt to burnish his reputation as an interpreter of Marxism; he resurrected an idea he had suggested in August 1917 and that he had touched upon in 1923, that the Soviet Union 'could be the country that blazes the trail to socialism'. The standard view of Marxist theorists had long been that a country – most notably Germany – that was far advanced in industrialization would take the lead in overthrowing capitalism and replace it with socialism. Other countries would then follow suit. The proletariat of a country as backward as Russia had not yet grown large enough or politically strong enough to deal a deathblow to capitalism. When Stalin first argued against these views, not many people paid much attention to him.

But much had changed in the Soviet Union as well as in the West. A party speaking for the proletariat ruled the Soviet Union, but in the West socialist parties showed no signs of attempting to topple capitalism. On the contrary, in some countries, and especially in Germany, the Social Democratic Party, founded on the principles of Marxism, had gone far to adopt revisionism, which called for a gradual, democratic path to socialism. Indeed, many leaders of the German Social Democratic Party rejected what they considered the undemocratic policies of the Bolsheviks, and in 1918 the radical wing of the party had separated from the movement and formed the German Communist Party, which could count on far fewer supporters than the Social Democrats. Similar splits had taken place in other Western European countries.

Patriotism had surely been a motive behind Stalin's unorthodox views on the future of socialism in the Soviet Union, which he advanced in his essay 'The October Revolution and the Tactics of the Russian Communists'. But political concerns were probably his main reasons for writing the article in 1924. In putting forth the doctrine that Russia could achieve socialism on its own, commonly known as the theory of 'socialism in one country', he was telling his countrymen that their efforts and suffering would not be in vain, that even if the Soviet Union remained alone in creating a new and egalitarian order it could survive and prosper. The country, he emphasized, was so rich in raw materials and the necessary human resources that it could reach the final goal on its own. As he put it in his essay, 'The victory of socialism is possible even in a country relatively undeveloped from the capitalist point of view'; and he claimed that Lenin, too, had held this position, which was not true. For many ordinary citizens that was irrelevant. The new doctrine bolstered the self-confidence of the masses, who had begun to fear that despite all their sacrifices they would never attain the final goal, socialism.

Stalin's advocacy of the doctrine of 'socialism in one country' is yet another sign of his political astuteness. He assured his readers that his views differed from those of Trotsky, who had, in fact, made a very similar argument during the Revolution of 1905. At that time, he had contended that the Russian proletariat had demonstrated greater energy and determination than their counterpart in Western Europe and would therefore be the pathfinder in the struggle for socialism. Stalin now called his rival's views 'a variety of Menshevism', a criticism that numerous party members considered to be devastating.

Many party leaders reacted to Stalin's doctrine with disbelief. No one was surprised that Trotsky, the target of so much criticism by Stalin and his supporters, now rejected a doctrine he had favored nineteen years earlier. He insisted that Stalin's position ran counter to one of his deepest convictions, that the ultimate goal of the Russian revolution, socialism, could not be reached in one country alone, and certainly not in a country as backward economically and socially as Russia. At the Fifteenth Conference of the Communist Party, held in 1926, Trotsky declared that 'I see no theoretical or political reason for thinking that we with our peasantry will find it easier to achieve socialism than the European proletariat will find it to seize power ... Even today I believe that the victory of socialism in our country can be safeguarded only together with a victorious revolution of the European proletariat.'

Other leading Marxists scoffed at Stalin's attempt to turn himself into a theorist, and David Riazanov, a noted scholar and director of the Marx-Engels Institute in Moscow, actually told him to his face that he was barking up the wrong tree. After listening to him espousing his theory at a party meeting, Riazanov went up to Stalin and urged him to abandon the doctrine: 'Stop it, Koba [one of Stalin's nicknames], don't make a fool of yourself. Everybody knows that theory is not exactly your field.'

Even Kamenev and Zinoviev, Stalin's supporters in the Politburo ever since Lenin became seriously ill, were taken aback by Stalin's doctrine. At first, they thought that he had formulated the notion of socialism in one country simply to highlight his differences with Trotsky and to produce a slogan that would appeal to the masses, which is precisely what happened. To Kamenev and Zinoviev it seemed to be a clever ploy, but when Stalin insisted that he was serious in advancing the idea of socialism in one country, the two men announced that they could not agree with him; they denounced the doctrine as an 'abandonment of traditional Bolshevism in favor of national communism'. As far as Stalin was concerned, the two colleagues were now his enemies, and he immediately sought new support in the Politburo, which had recently been enlarged. Three members of that body, Nikolai Bukharin, Alexei Rykov, and Mikhail Tomsky, declared their agreement with Stalin, who thus continued to enjoy the support of a majority in the highest organ of government.

The struggle for power now intensified exponentially. At the Fourteenth Party Congress in 1925, Kamenev responded in kind to attacks on him by Stalinists. He delivered a highly critical evaluation of the General Secretary, and bluntly declared that 'Comrade Stalin cannot perform the function of uniting the Bolshevik general staff ... We are against the doctrine of one-man rule, we are against the creation of a Leader.' But Stalin had made sure that most of the delegates would be his loyal supporters, and as soon as Kamenev had finished his speech cries of hostility were aimed at him: 'A lie! Humbug!' Other speakers who were known to be Stalin's opponents were drowned out with shouts by the delegates, and even Krupskaya, Lenin's wife, was met with hostile noise in the hall when she arrived on the podium. At one point, a number of delegates rose and began to chant 'Long live Comrade Stalin,' which was greeted with 'Loud and prolonged cheers. Cries of hurrah.' The Congress turned out to be a great success for Stalin, who once again sought to play the role of conciliator when he addressed the delegates. He wanted to give the impression of being above the fray and in the words of Robert Conquest, called for 'moderation and collective leadership'. But shortly after the Congress, Stalin indicated that his pose of moderation was staged to appeal to the delegates. He quickly arranged to have Kamenev's role in the Politburo reduced to 'candidate membership'. Stalin also saw to it that Mikhail Kalinin and Kliment Voroshilov, who had demonstrated their loyalty to the General Secretary, were promoted to full members of the highest organ of power.

MARSHAL KLIMENT VOROSHILOV (1881–1969)

Military specialists generally rate Voroshilov as a mediocre general but all agree that his political instincts and his sense of loyalty to Stalin were exemplary. He fought at Stalin's side in the Civil War during the Battle of Tsaritsyn in 1918 and despite the numerous mistakes of his leader he never swerved from loyalty to him. He understood Stalin, knew how to play up to him, and consequently managed to survive the political and judicial turmoil of the 1930s, at all times occupying a series of senior positions in the Communist Party and the Soviet government. To mention only a few of his achievements, he served on the Central Committee of the Communist Party from 1921 to 1961, he was a member of the Politburo from 1926 until 1960, he became the People's Commissar for Defense in 1934, and in 1935 he was appointed Marshal of the Soviet Union.

In return for these honors, he played a major role in the Great Terror and other atrocities of the 1930s. At the request of Stalin, in 1937 he denounced his colleagues in the military as traitors, claiming that they had formed a counterrevolutionary fascist organization; he based his accusation on false depositions submitted to the legal authorities handling the case. In 1940, he signed an order to Soviet officials to kill close to twenty thousand Polish citizens – military officers, as well as former government officials, landowners, industrialists and members of the intelligentsia – at Katyn. This is generally regarded as one of the most brutal massacres committed by the NKVD (Soviet secret police) during World War II. Only in 1990 did the authorities in Moscow acknowledge guilt for this carnage.

Voroshilov received many accolades for his loyalty to Stalin. But perhaps his greatest reward was that he was among the few top leaders during the 1930s who died, as one wit put it, the most unnatural of deaths in the Soviet Union during the Stalin era, a natural death. Voroshilov retired in 1960 and died nine years later at the age of eighty-eight.

By this time, in the mid–1920s, Stalin had taken many steps to solidify his hold on power. He had packed local party committees with his supporters and arranged the dismissal of thousands of so-called 'oppositionists', many of whom were now unemployed and destitute. In addition, he had secured control over the press and other sources of information. His henchmen saw to it that loyalists of Stalin were trucked to meetings of party members or of ordinary workers, throughout the country, with orders to disrupt any speaker who dared to criticize him or his supporters, and if that tactic failed, the speakers were to be ejected.

The opposition's attempts to stop Stalin from consolidating his position of preeminence often backfired. For example, in April 1926, Kamenev and Zinoviev, who had not been on speaking terms with Trotsky for three years, arranged a meeting with him to discuss the political situation. They revealed details of Stalin's intrigues and warned of his cunning and readiness to resort to the most ruthless measures to get his way. The three men stayed in touch and in the summer of 1926 formed a new organization that they named the 'United Opposition'. But very few party members rallied to their support, and in June Stalin unleashed a series of attacks on the United Opposition that undermined its potential effectiveness.

After he solidified his control of the Politburo by forming an alliance with Bukharin, Rykov, and Tomsky, Stalin arranged to have printed a letter that Lenin is supposed to have written but never published, in which he vilified Kamenev and Zinoviev as 'deserters of October' for having voted against his decision in 1917 to launch the proletarian revolution. Kamenev and Zinoviev retaliated by demanding that Lenin's testament, in which Stalin was severely criticized and belittled, be published. Not long before these conflicts, that document had been suppressed with the help of the two former allies of Stalin, and only recently had Trotsky and Krupskaya given in to pressure to deny its existence. Also, at roughly this time Stalin revealed in considerable detail the comments Kamenev and Zinoviev had made to him months earlier about Trotsky's nastiness. Stalin's aim, obviously, was to encourage party members to ask themselves how his two former allies, who not long ago had reviled Trotsky, could now cooperate with him in leading the United Opposition.

The mudslinging continued at a meeting of the Politburo in midsummer 1926, at which Stalin contended that the opposition was a 'Social Democratic deviation' and that its supporters must be forced to do more than promise to agree to be subject to party discipline; they must publicly recant their views. This demand was a violation of an agreement, to which Stalin had subscribed, not to force anyone to disavow his views. Trotsky, still a member of the Politburo, was enraged and, pointing at Stalin, he delivered a blistering charge: 'The First Secretary offers his candidature for the post of gravedigger of the Revolution!' Furious, Stalin barely managed to maintain his composure; he stalked out of the room but could not refrain from slamming the door. He soon took his revenge. A day later, he persuaded the Central Committee to remove Trotsky – who in 1925 had felt compelled to resign from the Commissariat of War – from the Politburo and to oust Kamenev from the position of candidate member.

Over the next two years, Stalin moved relentlessly to solidify his position as unchallengeable leader of the Communist Party. First, he arranged the expulsion of Trotsky, Kamenev, and Zinoviev from the Central Committee, which was a major institution in the formulation of national policies during the early period after the Revolution of 1917. When Trotsky and Zinoviev, on 7 November 1927, demonstrated their disapproval of Stalin by leading a separate group of their followers in celebrating the tenth anniversary of the Bolshevik Revolution, they were immediately punished with expulsion from the Communist Party. A month later, Stalin saw to it that seventy-five additional senior communists were expelled. But Stalin meted out the severest punishment to Trotsky, the man he feared and hated the most. In a decision that recalled the days of tsarist rule, he ordered the deportation of Trotsky to Alma Ata, a city near the Chinese border. A year later, Stalin banished Trotsky from the Soviet Union altogether, making it difficult for him to find a permanent residence. Western countries considered him a dangerous revolutionary and were not willing to offer him permanent asylum. For several years, he wandered from one country to another – first Turkey, then Norway, France, and finally, in 1937, Mexico, where the government granted him asylum. He now lived some 6,600 miles from Moscow, but that did not mean that he would escape the wrath of Stalin, as will be noted below.

Kamenev and Zinoviev, who seemed to have little difficulty changing their minds and their loyalties, now declared that Stalin's policies as well as his contention that the Soviet Union could reach socialism on its own were correct, and they avowed their loyalty to the man they had reviled a year earlier. They were readmitted to the party, but in the mid-1930s, when Stalin was the supreme and undisputed leader, he had his final revenge on the two men who had dared to oppose him.

In amassing his power, Stalin resorted to a variety of unorthodox methods that had never been used by Lenin against members of the Communist Party. He ordered his staff to tap the telephones of senior officials to find out their views on political developments and their plans in the upcoming political struggles. Stalin's staff also spent considerable time locating derogatory information on party people suspected of siding with the oppositionists. All along, Stalin maintained close contact with senior police officials to obtain information he could use against his enemies. It has been estimated that by 1930 over seven thousand Bolsheviks suspected of being sympathetic to the opposition had been exiled, imprisoned, or placed under police surveillance. Those who had been exiled lived under even worse conditions than those who had experienced a similar fate during the tsarist era.

The full meaning of Stalin's victory over all his rivals emerged clearly in 1929, when the country celebrated the leader's fiftieth birthday. (In the early 1920s, for reasons unknown, Stalin pushed the year of his birth forward by one year.) By this time, he had defeated the rightists in the Politburo in a fierce and lengthy political battle that will be discussed in detail in the next chapter. All that needs to be said at this point is that its outcome was such that Stalin could now feel free to rule the country as he saw fit. But before the events surrounding Stalin's birthday are described, it is worth noting that in 1920, when Lenin reached fifty, the celebration, in keeping with his wishes, was modest and in every respect restrained. The only souvenir that has been preserved is a pamphlet that ran to no more than thirty pages. There were no 'fawning eulogies', nor were there any speeches lauding the leader by party members who feared that they might be too restrained in praising the man who had inspired the Bolshevik Revolution and had then led the country through several crises that threatened to undermine the new order.

By contrast, on 21 December 1929, the entire country was swept up in a frenzy of excitement. Not many dared to abstain from the celebrations for the *khoziain* (boss), Stalin's unofficial title. All the Soviet newspapers devoted their entire issues to him that day, all displayed photographs of him, and innumerable articles focused on his outstanding abilities as a socialist leader. His bust could be seen in many places all over the country. He was hailed as the 'best Leninist', an 'iron Leninist', a 'great revolutionary', 'a granite Bolshevik', 'a man who never made a mistake', and as a 'superb success wherever he went during the civil war'. At every opportunity, Stalin stressed that he had been Lenin's right-hand man and his devoted disciple, claims that proved to be critical in legitimizing Stalin's desire to be the unchallengeable leader of the Soviet Union. Throughout the country, cities, streets, official buildings, and institutions were named for him; such accolades continued to be standard throughout his lifetime. He never discouraged these outpourings of praise because they reflected his wish to be acknowledged as the person who inspired all that was noble in Soviet life and beneficial to the country.

Pravda, the country's main newspaper, printed Stalin's statement of thanks to all who had sent greetings. It stressed his determination to devote all his energies to promoting the cause of socialism. It ran as follows:

> Your congratulations and greetings I place to the credit of the great party of the working class which bore me and reared me in its own image and likeness. It is precisely because I place them to the credit of our glorious Leninist party that I take bold to tender you my Bolshevik thanks.
>
> You need have no doubt, comrades, that I am prepared in the future, too, to devote to the cause of the working class, to the cause of the proletarian revolution and world Communism, all my strength, all my ability, and, if need be, all my blood, drop by drop.

The festivities in honor of Stalin's fiftieth birthday are historically important because they mark the beginning of the cult of personality, a central feature of Stalin's twenty-four-year rule, and of Stalinism, which many scholars now consider to be the best way to describe the totality of his policies. Within a few years of his fiftieth birthday, not only was Stalin hailed as a great political leader; he also became the final judge of truth in science and of the criteria to be used in judging art, literature, music, film, and linguistics, to mention only the major cultural spheres in which the 'boss' claimed that his judgement was superior to everyone else's.

Most important, under Stalin's rule the economic, political, and military institutions were transformed, turning the country into an industrial society and a major world power. But the transformation took place at the cost of horrendous suffering by the people of the Soviet Union. Not many dispassionate scholars are convinced that the latter was necessary to achieve the former.

5

'There Are No Fortresses Bolsheviks Cannot Storm'

Late in 1927, before Stalin's claim to preeminence in the Soviet Union had been sealed by the celebrations of his fiftieth birthday, the Communist Party's leadership had decided that the Soviet Union had to confront some fundamental questions concerning the national economy. To Stalin and his supporters, it seemed that the New Economic Policy, which in 1921 had ushered in a partial return to capitalism, had run its course and was no longer viable. To be sure, living conditions of most citizens had improved over the preceding six years, and now approached the level of 1913. Many peasants owned more land than in the pre-war years and most of them had made their peace with the new order. They still constituted about eighty percent of the total population and appeared to be fairly content. The peasants did not enjoy political freedom or civil rights, and they played no role in determining government policy, but they did not suffer from overbearing oppression. The ten years in power appeared to have had a moderating effect on the communists, who, it was widely assumed, would now concentrate on a gradual strengthening of the industrial sector of the economy.

But for a variety of reasons, Stalin had reached the conclusion that the country had no choice but to abandon the economic policies of the previous six years and adopt a program that would quickly transform the Soviet Union into an industrialized state and thus move the country closer to socialism. The working class would become the dominant force in society and it would welcome the abandonment of private ownership of property in the industrial and agrarian sectors of the economy. Industrialization would also strengthen the country militarily, a consideration touched upon below. Finally, there were purely economic developments that impelled Stalin to embark on a new course.

Agriculture, he noted, was in the doldrums. For example, in 1913 the Russian Empire exported close to ten million tons of grain, but by late 1925 that figure had dwindled to two million. The government claimed that peasants were deliberately withholding grain because they wanted to weaken the socialist government. In fact, the reason for the decline was quite different. In the pre-1913 period much of the surplus grain came from farms owned by landlords and, to a much lesser extent, by kulaks (the Russian word for 'fists'), peasants who were relatively well off.

But in the years immediately following the Revolution of 1917 landlords had been deprived of their land, which was then distributed to peasants. Although kulaks still played an important role in the countryside in the 1920s, they constituted no more than 3.9 percent of the peasant population, and despite all the vilification hurled at them by the Stalinists, they were not exactly wealthy landowners who exploited the masses of poor farmers. In 1927, the vast majority of kulaks owned two or three cows and generally no more than about twenty-eight acres of land suitable for farming. On average, a kulak family consisted of seven people, which further suggests that these maligned farmers were by no means rich. The real reason for the decline in grain exports was that a large number of peasants were now living somewhat better than had been the case prior to 1914. They had a bit more land at their disposal than during the tsarist era and they wished to reap the benefits. It is also worth noting that the richest peasants as a group earned only about fifty percent more than the poorest. It was misleading of Stalinists to charge the kulaks with exploitation of the vast majority of the people in the Soviet Union.

Stalin ignored these considerations because he needed a substantial increase in agricultural production to help finance his plan for rapid industrialization. To implement that plan, Russia would have to import machinery, for which the country would have to pay in agricultural products. Furthermore, as peasants moved to urban centers, there would be fewer farmers, who would need to be more productive to feed the growing number of city dwellers. It was a vicious circle that Soviet leaders believed could be broken only by greatly increasing the productivity of farms and reducing consumption, which would then leave enough capital for the development of industry. That consideration became an underlying principle of the government's economic policies after 1929.

Stalin and his supporters also spoke of the need to raise the cultural level of the citizens who made their living off the land. A majority of them were still illiterate, which meant, in effect, that a large percentage in the country could not function effectively in a modern economy. Moreover, seventy-five percent of the peasants still lived in communes, the dominant local institutions in pre-1917 Russia, which controlled local education, among other things, and, in the view of many officials, did not function efficiently. Soviet leaders were troubled by the fact that ten years after the Bolshevik Revolution, the communes were more important centers of administration than the soviets or the cooperatives, both favored by the Bolsheviks. The statistics on this point are revealing. In 1927, the 2,300 soviets in the countryside disposed of a budget of about sixty million rubles, whereas the budgets of various peasant associations in the entire country amounted to about eighty million rubles. Perhaps most troubling to the Stalinists, the kulaks tended to be the leaders of local organizations, and the authorities in Moscow feared that if their wings were not clipped, they would in time develop into a force capable of challenging the government.

The Stalinists were further concerned about the peasants' failure to abandon their devotion to the Orthodox Church, which to communists symbolized 'the rot of tsarism'. In 1928 alone, some 560 new communities of Orthodox believers were formed, and in the Ukraine the number of priests greatly increased. Bolsheviks took their atheism seriously and were committed to rooting out all religions.

The fear of attack by foreign countries was yet another concern of the government that underlay its determination to industrialize rapidly and turn the country into a major military power. Stalin and his followers contended that capitalist countries would once again wage war against the Soviet Union in order to root out socialism, which they had attempted to do only a decade earlier during the Civil War, when several countries had sent troops to Russia to help the counterrevolutionaries. The favorite formulation of this fear was that the Soviet Union faced a hostile capitalist world surrounding the one socialist country, or in the language of that time, the socialist state had to contend with 'capitalist encirclement'. But there was a more specific concern about a possible attack. In 1926, relations between the Soviet Union and Great Britain had become especially tense, because British coal miners, who were engaged in a bitter strike, had been openly supported by the Soviet government – including, according to some accounts, receiving financial support. In 1927, Britain broke off all relations with the Soviet Union.

The evidence in support of radical economic and social change appeared to be overwhelming when the subject was raised at various Communist Party meetings in the Soviet Union. But the debates on this subject at the very highest levels of the party were intense, and the opponents of Stalin eventually paid dearly for their rejection of his ideas. When the debates over the economic future of the Soviet Union began, Stalin had not yet fully revealed his inability to tolerate anyone who dared to disagree with him. He took his ideological commitments very seriously, but those commitments were closely interwoven with his self-esteem, his ego. He regarded any opposition to his views as equivalent to betrayal, and he rarely failed to deal harshly with anyone who dared to question his supreme authority.

In 1927, Bukharin, one of the most interesting and thoughtful leaders of the Bolshevik movement, led the opposition to Stalin's economic plans. Even though he had belonged to the far-left wing of the party in the revolutionary period and had opposed the Treaty of Brest-Litovsk in the belief that it was unnecessary, because the revolution would soon break out in Germany and other European countries, Lenin thought highly of him. In his testament, Lenin referred to Bukharin as 'the most valuable and biggest theoretician of the Party' despite voicing some reservations about him. He believed that Bukharin's 'theoretical views can only with the very greatest doubt be regarded as fully Marxist for there is something scholastic in him (he has never learned, and I think never fully understood, the dialectic).' Lenin may have exaggerated Bukharin's weakness as a thinker, but he seems to have understood that Bukharin could not be counted on to toe the line on the issue of how to advance the cause of socialism. He was at least an independent thinker.

He demonstrated that quality fully in 1928, when he opposed Stalin's proposals for abandoning the New Economic Policy and adopting a radically new direction, which in some ways was not as new as depicted. In many respects, though not entirely, Stalin was advocating a return to War Communism, the policies that dominated the economic thinking of Lenin in the years from 1918 to 1921, that is, strict control by Moscow over all branches of the economy. Bukharin, now the leader of what was considered the right-wing opposition, argued vigorously against the abandonment of the New Economic Policy. It was a bold shift for him; a few years earlier he had supported Stalin in his struggle against the Left Opposition.

Bukharin now made overtures to Kamenev, his former enemy, but he knew that he was treading in dangerous waters. He visited Kamenev to discuss Stalin's economic program, but before saying anything of substance he urged his host to be cautious: 'Do not let anyone know of our meeting. Do not telephone; it is overheard. The G.P.U. [secret police] is following me and watching you also.' He then told Kamenev that he considered 'Stalin's line fatal to the revolution. This line is leading to the abyss. Our disagreements with Stalin are far, far more serious than those we have with you.' And Bukharin revealed that 'for several weeks, I have refused to speak to Stalin. *He is an unprincipled intriguer who subordinates everything to his appetite for power.* At any given moment he will change his theories in order to get rid of someone.' The contacts he had had with Stalin over the last months, he continued, had been reduced to exchanging insults. Bukharin had concluded that one could not trust Stalin 'with the smallest document'. When he addressed the Politburo, he took special precautions not to let the text leave his hands for fear that if Stalin got hold of it he would alter it to suit his designs to besmirch him.

Bukharin opposed Stalin's economic program of rapid industrialization because he was convinced that it could be implemented only by increasing taxes on private enterprises and private peasants, which would wreak havoc on the already-precarious economy and possibly restore the hardships endured by the country during the period of War Communism. He went so far as to warn that Stalin's plan would lead to 'military-feudal exploitation' of the peasantry. Instead of taking this route, the government should adopt the slogan 'enrich yourselves', which harked back to the days of F. P. Guizot, the prime minister of France in 1847–8, who gave that advice to citizens interested in securing the vote. In Bukharin's view, so long as the communists controlled industry, transportation, and banking, as they did, there was no danger that his proposals, if adopted, would undermine socialism. In contrast to the Left, Bukharin now discounted the likelihood of revolutions in the West in the foreseeable future. In his view, the Soviet Union had to concentrate on building 'socialism in one country', an idea he had hinted at even before Stalin took up this theme. On another occasion, in July 1928, he warned that collectivization of peasant farmers would lead to mass violence in the countryside. Stalin was not fazed; he insisted that to achieve socialism it would be necessary to step up class warfare. Shocked by Stalin's callousness, Bukharin began to refer to him as Genghis Khan, a reference to the brutal Mongol who early in the thirteenth century conquered large parts of what came to be Russia and in the process massacred untold numbers of innocent people.

There is little question that the assertion of his power was a central motive in Stalin's battles with other leaders of the Bolshevik party, but it would be a mistake to belittle his ideological commitment to socialism. He believed that the changes he wished to introduce would lead the country to a realization of the final goal as envisioned by Marx and Lenin. He made his fervor on this subject absolutely clear. 'We are fifty or a hundred years behind the advanced countries,' he declared in 1931. 'We must make good this lag in ten years. Either we do it or they crush us.' And he did not doubt that as a result of his economic policies the Soviet Union would soon overtake the West economically. Two years earlier, in 1929, he had made the same point perhaps even more passionately and certainly more boastfully: 'When we have the USSR in an automobile, and the muzhik [peasant] on a tractor, let the capitalist gentlemen, who boast so loudly of their "civilization", try to overtake us! We shall see then which countries are to be classified as backward and which as advanced.' Most people in Stalin's inner circle were convinced that he believed his own rhetoric.

Stalin never lost faith in the correctness of his policies for the attainment of socialism or in the conviction that only he could lead the country to that goal, whose success would require methods of rule that he and only he understood to be necessary and appropriate. Whether or not those methods violated the conventional norms of morality did not concern him. Put differently, he never doubted that the ends justified the means.

It has been argued that Stalin's economic policies amounted to a second revolution, or, as it is often called, a revolution from above. As such, it was different from the generally accepted definition of revolution, namely, a fundamental change in the exercise of sovereignty, as occurred, for example, during the French Revolution of 1789. During that upheaval, the monarchy was overthrown and political power was seized by leaders of the bourgeoisie, or middle class. There was no such change in the Soviet Union in 1928, when Stalin assumed leadership of the Communist Party. As he himself claimed, he was committed to implementing the ideas of Lenin, who had led the Revolution of 1917. What Stalin accomplished in 1928 was the abandonment of the New Economic Policy, adopted by Lenin in 1921 because his initial program, War Communism, had failed to produce a revival of the Soviet economy, which had been severely damaged during World War I and the Civil War.

Trotsky offered a different name for the changes that took place in the years from 1929 to the late 1930s. He harked back to the revolutionary period in the 1790s, and characterized Stalin's policies as a 'Thermidorian Revolution', a term used to describe the overthrow of Maximilien Robespierre, the radical leader who had introduced social and political changes and, in addition, had established a regime of terror against opponents of his rule. But Trotsky's designation of Stalin's program is misleading because the Soviet leader did not intend to abandon the social and political program of his predecessor, Lenin.

Moreover, a committed Marxist might argue that far from staging a counterrevolution, Stalin carried out a revolution by transforming the superstructure, that is, he changed the ideas, values and beliefs of the people in the Soviet Union. In doing so, Stalin created the foundations for a radically new economic system. Once that had been achieved, a Marxist would contend, the political system would also be transformed. Thus, it might be more accurate to designate the economic and social changes that Stalin imposed on the Soviet Union as the completion, albeit in ways not initially anticipated, of the Revolution of 1917.

Stalin was certainly more authoritarian and far more brutal than the founder of Bolshevism. But, of course, Lenin longed for socialism, and he was not squeamish about resorting to force to crush the opponents of his ultimate goal, as he demonstrated in the years immediately after the Bolshevik seizure of power. He made his most forceful argument for terror in an article he wrote in January 1918 but which was not published in *Pravda* until January 1929. In that article, Lenin called for a variety of means to achieve

> the common aim – to clean the land of Russia of all sorts of vermin, of fleas, of bedbugs – the rich, and so on and so forth. In one place half a score of rich, a dozen crooks, half a dozen workers who shirk their work ... will be put in prison. In another place they will be put to cleaning latrines. In a third place they will be provided with 'yellow tickets' after they have served their time, so that all people shall have them under surveillance, as harmful persons, until they reform. In a fourth place, one out of every ten idlers will be shot on the spot. In a fifth place, mixed methods may be adopted ... The more variety there will be, the better and richer will be our experience, the more certain and rapid will be the success of socialism.

In Lenin's view, *'weakness, hesitation, or sentimentality ... would be a great crime to Socialism.'*

Although Stalin's ideological commitments were virtually identical to those of Lenin, his persona differed sharply from that of his mentor. Those differences were decisive in shaping Stalin's conduct not only toward colleagues, rivals, and subordinates in the Communist Party, but also toward his family and assumed friends. Stalin was a man with a huge ego who expected to be venerated and could not brook any criticism – certainly not of his plans to improve the lot of the Russian people. His daughter, Svetlana Alliluyeva, who suffered a complicated relationship with her father, pointed out that he 'could not tolerate the slightest attempt to change his mind about anybody ... [he] was constitutionally incapable of reversing a decision he had reached about a person whom he suspected of being an enemy, even if that person had once been a friend ... Any attempt to persuade him [to change his mind] ... only made him furious.'

Stalin was also given to outbursts of anger that can only be characterized as maniacal. An incident revealed by Svetlana in an interview with the historian Robert Tucker dramatically demonstrates this trait. Stalin was in the habit of pacing back and forth in his Kremlin apartment as he contemplated how to handle political or other problems, and occasionally he would spit on the floor. 'Once, the parrot (that was caged in one of the rooms) imitated him spitting. Incensed rather than amused, Stalin reached into the cage with his pipe [invariably in his mouth as he took his walks] and killed the bird with a blow to its head.' He could not tolerate any sign of disrespect, not even from a small, harmless bird.

When the Five Year Plan was officially announced in October 1928, the details of the government's aims were staggering. The Politburo had charged *Gosplan* (the State Planning Commission, established in 1921) with the task of drawing up a detailed plan for restructuring the economy. It was a monumental assignment, and Gosplan obliged by formulating a precise, all-embracing, and startlingly ambitious set of goals. Few responsible economists not driven by political pressure would dare to undertake such a task. Generally, economists are pleased if their predictions of economic trends from one month or one year to the next turn out to be more or less accurate. But Gosplan did not hesitate to follow orders, and agreed to devise a plan whose key provisions were designed to industrialize the country quickly and turn every worker in the Soviet Union into an employee of the state. For a true believer in socialism, no goals were more sacrosanct.

Gosplan's formula specified the precise targets for every sector of the economy, all of them to be achieved in five years. Industry as a whole was to increase production by 235.9 percent; heavy industry was assigned an even larger increase, 279.2 percent. Output of pig iron was to be virtually doubled, and electric power was to increase fourfold. Agriculture was assigned a more moderate increase, 150 percent. In addition, the government announced that the cost of industrial goods would be reduced by thirty-five percent, but wholesale prices would be reduced by only twenty-four percent, leaving a substantial profit for investment. Within two years, in June 1930, the government's enthusiasm for its program reached the level of euphoria. Even though it had become evident that unrealistic targets had been projected, Stalin proclaimed that the plan would be fulfilled in four years, not five.

In several respects, the projections for the countryside were even more ambitious than the plan for industrialization, and more likely to encounter resistance as well as failures. As already mentioned, the aim in the agrarian sectors of the country was in good measure ideological, to transform peasants from property owners into workers for the state. Achieving this goal meant uprooting close to eighty percent of the population, roughly 130 million people (counting children). The authorities knew that the peasants, who were economically and emotionally deeply attached to their landholdings, would resist the government's plans. Indeed, many of them were convinced that the government intended to reestablish some form of serfdom in the rural areas of the Soviet Union, the despised social system that had been abolished in 1861.

Gosplan initially opted for gradual collectivization of farms, so as to ease the pain on peasants. But in 1929 Stalin chose to speed up the process. It may be that once the government's ambitious industrial plans had been made public, senior officials, or Stalin himself, decided that the campaign in the countryside must proceed at a faster pace; it was, after all, the only way that Gosplan could secure both enough capital and the additional workers needed for rapid expansion of the industrial sector.

A central feature of the Five Year Plan was to abolish individual farms quickly and replace them with collective farms, which, the authorities predicted, would be much more efficient than the small, privately owned farms. Far fewer workers would thus be needed to produce an adequate food supply for the country and even a surplus for export that could be sold in exchange for machinery. The agricultural laborers no longer employed in the countryside would move to the cities to work in the new industries that were being established.

The campaign in the countryside proved to be an assault on a majority of the population that caused enormous economic losses and horrendous pain to ordinary people, whose one wish was to be left alone. As already noted, Stalin and his associates expected resistance from the peasants, and made careful preparations to deal with it. They sent many thousands of officials into the countryside with orders to 'liquidate the Kulaks as a class' and to pressure the rest of the population to join collective farms. The government did not divulge its intentions with regard to the kulaks, a group that numbered roughly two million adults and eight million children. They were considered too hostile to collectives and many were therefore deported to distant places in the Far East.

In numerous parts of the country, as the peasants realized that the authorities would use force to drive them into the collectives, they mounted fierce opposition that included killing government agents who implemented the government's plans. Soldiers who accompanied the agents were under orders to spare no efforts to crush the rebels, and as a result many localities were transformed into battlefields. In a fair number of places, government forces armed with machine guns surrounded the villagers, who faced the choice of death or submission. The land, homes, and tools of ordinary peasants and kulaks were confiscated and turned into collective farms.

The historian Isaac Deutscher was in the Ukraine during this period and while traveling in a railway car he met a colonel of the secret police, completely broken in spirit by the violence. 'Almost sobbing,' he told Deutscher that 'I worked in the underground against the Tsar and then I fought in the civil war. Did I do all that in order that I should now surround villages with machine-guns and order my men to fire indiscriminately into crowds of peasants? Oh, no, no!'

In his excellent book *The First Socialist Society*, Geoffrey Hosking cites the recollections of Victor Kravchenko, a party emissary in the countryside, who also described the suffering of the peasants. He saw one woman deliberately burning her home as she cried: 'Infidels! Murderers! We've worked all our lives for our home. You won't have it. The flames shall have it.' Kravchenko also revealed that he was urged by senior officials to 'pump ... [the grain] out of them, wherever it's hidden ... Don't be afraid of taking extreme measures. The party stands full-square behind you. Comrade Stalin expects it.'

On entering a village in Dnepropetrovsk oblast (an administrative region), Kravchenko was amazed by the total silence in the place. 'All the dogs have been eaten,' he was told by one of the few people left there. 'We've eaten everything we could lay our hands on – cats, dogs, field mice, birds. When it's light tomorrow, you will see that the trees have been stripped of their bark, for that too has been eaten.'

Many peasants, having somehow learned that government officials and soldiers were about to descend on their villages, decided to leave as little as possible of their livestock and crops to be taken. If they were going to be robbed of their possessions, the peasants decided, they would have a last fling. They slaughtered many of their animals and treated themselves to elaborate meals that they would normally have shunned as extravagant. In numerous regions, they burned their crops simply out of spite.

The losses in human lives and economic resources that resulted from what was later referred to as a 'military operation, a cruel civil war', were enormous. During the period of collectivization, slightly more than half of all the horses were killed; roughly forty-five percent of the one hundred million large cattle met the same fate. Two thirds of the country's sheep and goats were slaughtered. In addition, because of the chaotic conditions in the countryside, huge areas of land remained fallow. As early as February 1929, the government realized that the country faced serious shortages of food, and to cope with that crisis it introduced rationing, which meant that urban dwellers, too, felt the sting of collectivization.

The government never released accurate statistics on the economic and human losses caused by the program of collectivization, let alone by official actions that were utterly unreasonable. In 1932, for example, Stalin demanded that farmers in the Ukraine produce unprecedented quantities of grain for export to acquire funds to be used to finance rapid industrialization. The authorities also used some of the grain to feed city dwellers and the army. The annual increase in the sale of grain – at surprisingly low prices, it should be noted – was very high. In the mid-1920s, the Soviet Union exported 2 million metric tons a year, but in 1931 that figure rose to 5.1 million, which resulted in severe food shortages in such areas as the Ukraine, the northern Caucasus, the Volga region, Kazakhstan, and the West Siberian Plain. In some areas, the plight of the local population was so dire that some people resorted to cannibalism.

Scholars are generally agreed that all told about five million peasants lost their lives during the implementation of the agrarian policy, and one important student of the subject, Moshe Lewin, suggested that the true figure might be as high as ten million. An official who had participated in enforcing the government's program in the Ukraine later gave the following account of what he witnessed and how it affected him: 'Here I saw people dying in solitude by slow degrees, dying hideously. They had been trapped and left to starve, each in his home, by a political decision made in a far-off capital around conference and banquet tables. There was not even the consolation of inevitability to relieve the horror.' Some kulaks were so distressed that they killed their families and then committed suicide.

At first, Stalin denied all reports of famine, but in February 1930 he realized that the campaign in the countryside had aroused such deep discontent that the entire Five Year Plan might be in jeopardy. By that time, about fifty percent of all peasant households had been collectivized, but the brutality of government officials had been so fierce that Stalin considered it necessary to take a step back. On 2 March 1930, he published an article, 'Dizzy with Success', in *Pravda*, the most authoritative newspaper in the country, in which he declared, contrary to a conviction he had stated unequivocally in 1928, that collectivization could not be imposed by force. He blamed the violence and chaos in the villages on the excessive zeal of lower-ranking Communist Party officials. The successes already achieved, he declared, 'sometimes induce a spirit of vanity and conceit: "We can do anything!" There is nothing we can't do. People not infrequently become intoxicated by such successes; they become dizzy with success, lose all sense of proportion and the capacity to understand realities; they show a tendency to overrate their own strength and to underrate the strength of the enemy; adventurist attempts are made to solve all questions of socialist construction "in a trice".' Toward the end of the article, he struck a note of moderation, which was out of keeping with the statements he had made two years earlier in advocating his radical policies. 'The art of leadership,' he said, 'is a serious matter. One must not lag behind the movement, because to do so is to lose contact with the masses. But neither must one run too far ahead, because to run too far ahead is to lose the masses and to isolate oneself. He who wants to lead a movement and at the same time keep in touch with the masses must wage a fight on two fronts – against those who lag behind and against those who run too far ahead.'

The government now changed course; it issued a decree allowing peasants to leave the collectives, and the reaction was swift. Within about eight weeks the number of peasant families in collectives dropped from fourteen to six million. Yet a few months later, the government resumed the process of collectivization, though at a slower pace. By 1932, sixty percent of all peasant families belonged to collectives, still a radical change imposed on millions of people within a short period of about three years.

Sensing the enormity of the turbulence and suffering in the countryside, Stalin made some additional concessions to peasants. Instead of forcing them into the preferred type of collective, the state farm (*sovkhoz*), in which peasants worked full-time on the commonly held land, the government gave them the option of entering a *kolkhoz* (collective farm), in which peasants divided their working time between their privately held small plots and the land controlled by the collective. In addition, peasants in *kolkhozy* were permitted to own a few pigs or sheep, one cow, and an unspecified number of poultry. Most collectives fell into this latter category, an outcome unwelcome in official circles because it demonstrated the effectiveness of economic incentives. Russian peasants were not well educated, but they were not stupid. Peasants in the *kolkhozy* would work leisurely during the sixty to one hundred days they devoted to the fully collectivized land and conserve their energies for their own plots, the proceeds of which they could sell directly to consumers.

It was only at the end of the 1930s that the harvests of the country's farmers surpassed those of the late 1920s. Still, for the next five decades, until the collapse of the Soviet Union in 1991, agricultural productivity remained low, as did the quality of food products. Moreover, since the transportation system was primitive, a significant percentage of the agrarian produce rotted before it ever reached the market. The consensus among historians of the Soviet Union and economists who have studied the Five Year Plans is that Stalin's agrarian policies were a catastrophic failure.

The implementation of Stalin's plan for rapid industrialization of the Soviet Union proved to be much less bloody than the plan for the agrarian sector of the economy, and its achievements were in many respects more impressive. But there were also many setbacks, and the final results were far from the ideals of the theorists of Marxism and especially of Lenin, who had envisioned a society in which the proletariat would prosper as free citizens.

By the mid-1930s, the government could boast of having developed entirely new industries that produced tractors, automobiles, agricultural machinery, and airplanes. Entire cities devoted primarily to industry had been created. Two of the most notable examples of new urban centers created as a result of the various Five Year Plans are Komsomolsk-on-Amur, in the Far East, and Magnitogorsk, on the Siberian side of the Ural Mountains. Perhaps the most striking statistic in support of the government's claim of success is that within twelve years the labor force in industry, construction, and transport had risen from 4.6 million in 1928 to 12.6 million in 1940, an increase of close to 300 percent. Soviet economists added another 10.2 million office workers of various kinds to the statistics, enabling them to claim that the number of proletarians had risen to 22.8 million. Another measure of the extent of the change in the economy is indicated by the fact that between 1928 and 1932 industrial output rose from forty-eight percent to seventy percent of the country's total production of goods. These increases were welcomed not only as an economic achievement but also as a major ideological advance because they signified solid growth of the working class, considered the backbone of a socialist society.

But industrialization did not proceed smoothly and the burgeoning working class did not enjoy the fruits of their labor, to use the terminology of a famous Marxist prediction. The economic surge turned out to be chaotic and often ineffective; in some regions the authorities had numerous factories built, only to find that there were not enough machines for them to begin production. And frequently, the new enterprises that were well stocked with machines lacked enough skilled workers to run them. Despite claims by the government, none of the projected goals were reached, and in several sectors of the economy the shortfalls were significant.

For the workers who manned the new factories, the greatest disappointment was the conditions under which they were obliged to work. They were so burdensome that workers often sought and found better jobs. In the coal and mining industries workers were so badly treated that the average length of time people stayed at their jobs was four months. Such high turnover made it difficult for managers to maximize productivity. In 1932, the government adopted drastic measures to prevent the constant movement by workers from one enterprise to another. Every worker was required to acquire an 'internal passport' and, in addition, a 'dwelling permit'. As soon as a person moved to another city, he or she had to register with the local police, whose permission workers needed to settle in a new locality. The passport system was designed both to keep workers at their place of work and to enable the police to maintain control over the country's citizens.

In addition, each worker received a 'wage book', known after 1938 as a 'work book', that employees always had to carry with them. Factory supervisors would record any violation of discipline in these books, and the rules governing workers' conduct were extremely rigorous. For example, an employee who failed to show up for work for one day without a reason considered legitimate by the authorities could be dismissed, which did not simply mean loss of a job; the punishment could and often did include loss of living quarters. In 1939, the government issued a new definition of absenteeism: a worker who was late by twenty minutes or more without a valid reason was considered absent for the day. In 1940, the authorities defined absenteeism as a criminal offense punishable by six months of 'corrective labor', which meant that the worker could remain at his job but at a cut in pay of twenty-five percent. A worker dismissed from his job was deemed to have committed a crime, for which the punishment would generally be a jail sentence.

Workers were poorly paid and they struggled to keep their heads above water. Most working-class families lived in one room in an apartment, sharing cooking and bathroom facilities with several other families. In other words, a four-room apartment would generally accommodate four families. On average, a worker in Moscow in the 1930s occupied less than three square meters (about thirty-two square feet) of space. Food was relatively inexpensive, but its quality was low. Most galling of all to ordinary workers was the inequality of economic rewards for different categories of employees. During Lenin's leadership of the Soviet Union no member of the Communist Party, not even those who occupied top positions, earned more than a skilled worker.

But in June 1931, Stalin changed that policy, and he offered an argument against equal pay for all employees that one would expect from a committed capitalist: that progress in industrialization could be achieved only if employees were rewarded according to their performance. Only by offering higher pay to the skilled and dedicated workers, he insisted, would it be possible to prod employees into improving their skills and to promote efficiency in the workplace. At the Seventeenth Party Congress in 1934, Stalin offered an especially vigorous defense of this policy: equal pay, he declared, was a 'reactionary, petty-bourgeois absurdity worthy of a primitive sect of ascetics but not of a Socialist society organized on Marxist lines'. He went on to declare that only 'leftist blockheads ... idealize the poor as the eternal bulwark of Bolshevism'. He also dismissed the notion of 'equalization of pay ... [as] petty bourgeois prejudice'. In referring to Marx, Stalin had in mind the former's prediction that initially workers in a classless society would be compensated not according to their needs but according to their labor. Yet the differences in pay in the Soviet Union, as well as the differences in other forms of compensation, were so large that they clearly violated the spirit of Marxism and, even more so, of Bolshevism.

For example, the pay of well-trained engineers was between four and eight times as much as that of an ordinary worker. Employees who held administrative positions could earn up to thirty times as much as workers in the bottom rank. In 1935, the government introduced a new category of workers, the Stakhanovites, who earned considerably more than most laborers. The origins of this category throw further light on the manipulations of the government to press employees into working harder. Alexei Stakhanov, a coal miner in the Donbass, was carefully primed to be more productive than everyone else. Before he began working on 21 August, he was well rested and well fed, and some of the work a single miner would normally do was assigned to others, but these special arrangements were not generally known. All the newspapers claimed that, to universal amazement, in one six-hour shift Stakhanov managed to dig 102 tons of coal from the Stalin Central Mine, sixteen times as much as any previous miner. *Pravda* glowingly publicized his feat and it was designated the official target for other workers. From that time, many workers aspired to match the hero's achievements and thus join the ranks of the elite Stakhanovites, who were rewarded with higher pay and more comfortable apartments than those assigned to average achievers. To encourage workers to emulate the Stakhanovites, Soviet newspapers adopted the following slogan: 'There are no fortresses Bolsheviks cannot storm.'

In 1977, Stakhanov published *The Story of My Life*, in which he paid tribute to Stalin:

> When I remember it all, when I collect my thoughts together, every time I want to say just one thing: thank you, Comrade Stalin! Comrade Stalin gave me, an ordinary worker, more support than I could ever have imagined. I am now used to the expression, 'the Stakhanovite movement'. I often see my name in the papers, and hear it spoken at meetings. Frankly, at first I couldn't understand it all. But now I think it's right to call our movement Stalinist, because it was the working class, which is on the move in the Stalinist campaign for technological advance that created my record and those of my comrades. It was Comrade Stalin who made our movement a broad one.

Not all of Stakhanov's colleagues were pleased by what appeared to be a stunning performance. They resented being pressured to work harder, to emulate him, and some evidence has emerged that they lynched a few of his followers. In response to the protests, the government changed course slightly: it now lauded a new category of workers, the so-called rationalizers, who proposed more effective ways of increasing production.

In the 1930s, another preferred group, the *nomenklatura* (list), became more numerous and enjoyed far more privileges than ever before. This category had originated in 1922, when Stalin rose to the position of General Secretary, and it consisted of party leaders and prominent persons who occupied important administrative positions in the government, the economy, the military services, education, and culture. Selection for this elite group required the approval of the Communist Party. To critics of Soviet communism, it seemed that the nomenklatura represented a new ruling class similar to the elites in capitalist countries.

Although the wealth of the Soviet elite did not match that of Western capitalists, there is merit to this comparison. Members of the nomenklatura were very well paid and the government bestowed many honors as well as special privileges on them. They lived in spacious and comfortable apartments; they had access to dachas (country homes), where they would spend weekends and longer periods during the summer; they ate their meals on workdays in dining rooms inaccessible to ordinary workers; and they could spend time at rest homes if they needed to get away from the tensions of work. Senior officials and administrators were provided with cars driven by chauffeurs. And every member of the nomenklatura could shop at special stores well stocked with low-priced food and other goods that were not available to the rest of the population. The authorities made extensive efforts to conceal these stores, placing them on out-of-the-way streets. Entrance was reserved for citizens with a special identity card. But many people knew where they were – a local citizen pointed one out to me when I visited Moscow in 1973 – and they knew what kind of business was conducted in them. Their resentment at suffering such discrimination was evident to anyone with whom they spoke candidly.

At the height of the economic turbulence in November 1932, Stalin suffered a horrendous personal blow. His wife Nadezhda Alliluyeva committed suicide after a stormy public exchange with Stalin. His first wife, as noted earlier, had died in 1907 and ten years later he married Nadezhda, who was seventeen, twenty-three years younger than he. According to Stalin's daughter, Svetlana, a legend was told that Stalin had met Nadezhda when she was only two years old and that he had rescued her from drowning in a river. She was the daughter of a worker who supported Bolshevism, so her credentials were sound. Svetlana's recollections of her mother in many ways portray an appealing person: 'Mother was very much loved by everyone,' she noted in her autobiographical sketches. 'She was intelligent, beautiful, extraordinarily gentle and considerate in every relationship. At the same time, she could be firm, stubborn and unyielding when she felt that a conviction could not be compromised. She was the acknowledged head of the household.' She was also a fervent supporter of Bolshevism and, in Tucker's words, idolized her husband as the 'embodiment of the Revolution'. She gave birth to two children, Vasily and Svetlana, and although Stalin was too self-centered to be an easy man to live with, the marriage seemed reasonably successful. There is evidence, however, that on one occasion she tried to leave him. The two were known to have occasionally engaged in nasty disputes, and it is likely that Stalin, who could lose his temper, at times behaved badly toward her.

In the early 1930s, Nadezhda began to have serious doubts about the drift of her husband's policies, and according to some sources, she underwent some sort of psychological collapse. In the late 1920s, she had gone to Berlin to visit her brother and at that time she consulted a neurologist. Not much is known about her mental health, but her family did have a history of psychological problems – her brother and sister suffered from depression. One month before her suicide, she had told her sister that she also suffered from depression. At about the same time, she had indicated, according to Svetlana, that 'she was sick of everything,' 'everything bored her,' and 'nothing made her happy,' not even her children.

On 8 November 1932, Stalin and Nadezhda attended a celebration of the fifteenth anniversary of the Bolshevik Revolution at the Kremlin home of Marshal Voroshilov. At one point during the festivities, Stalin turned to Nadezhda and made the following comment: 'Hey, you, have a drink.' He then threw a cigarette into his wine glass and shoved it at her across the table. Infuriated,

Nadezhda shouted, 'Don't you dare "hey" me!' and immediately left the room. She went to her bedroom in the Kremlin and the next morning was found lifeless; she had shot herself with a small revolver that her brother had given her as a gift. Svetlana recalled in her autobiographical letters that her mother left Stalin 'a terrible letter, full of reproaches and accusations. It wasn't purely personal; it was partly political as well.'

Svetlana related that her father was 'deeply shaken'. He could not understand why his wife had committed suicide and was convinced that 'in her heart she had been on the side of the opposition to him.' He could not forgive her for having abandoned him. At the 'civil leave-taking ceremony he went up to the coffin for a moment. Suddenly he pushed it away from him, turned on his heel and left. He didn't even go to the funeral.' Persuaded that Nadezhda had 'left him as his personal enemy', he never visited her graveside. He told some of his colleagues that 'he didn't want to go on living either.'

In his *Portrait de Staline*, Victor Serge reported that Stalin was so distressed that at a meeting of the Politburo he submitted his resignation. The members of the committee, all of them his faithful supporters, did not think he meant it and no one dared to accept his offer to leave office. Anyone who had done so 'would have risked a lot. Nobody stirred ... At last Molotov said: Stop it, stop it. You have got the party's confidence ... The incident was closed.'

The death of Stalin's wife had a strong impact on him; he became something of a recluse. He left the apartment that he and Nadezhda had occupied and moved to a smaller place in the Kremlin that did not stir up any memories of his wife.

6

The Great Terror, 1936–1938

The more secure Stalin was as leader of the Communist Party and the Soviet Union, the more insecure he became about his political future and even his personal safety. He had persuaded himself that he faced numerous enemies in high places who were determined to oust him from his position of power. As a result, he trusted only a few people, and in the mid-1930s their number kept declining. Even members of his family, close friends, officials who had served the country for years, and senior officers in the armed services with distinguished records fell under suspicion of being hostile to him.

Not only did Stalin fear political conspiracies by opponents seeking to muster enough votes to defeat him in the Politburo or the Central Committee of the Communist Party. He also feared that his enemies were planning to assassinate him. Every time he left the Kremlin for his favorite dacha in Kuntsevo he would wait until the last moment before his departure to give his chauffeur and bodyguards instructions on which route to take. A high fence and barricades surrounded the country home, which was also carefully guarded by elite soldiers specially trained to keep an eye out for intruders. Land mines had been planted in the woods near the dacha to prevent strangers from approaching the leader's home.

Stalin considered it his duty to deal harshly with those whom he considered his 'enemies', who almost invariably were also denounced as 'enemies of the people'. The vast majority of these citizens – the total number reached millions – never received a trial and some of those who did were subjected to 'show trials' in which the outcome was predetermined; often, the accused had been tortured until agreeing to plead guilty.

The state terror against the citizens of the Soviet Union, initiated in mid-1934, consisted of three major features: the show trials of leading Bolsheviks and senior army officers, purges of a vast number of Communist Party members, and the arrest of ordinary citizens suspected of hostility to Bolshevism. Although the targets of the three campaigns of terror differed, the purpose of them all was identical: to bolster Stalin's claim of omnipotence and to assure the realization of his concept of socialism.

Some historians, most notably Professor Terry Martin, have suggested that the policy of ethnic cleansing, which was originally implemented in the 1920s and reached a high point immediately after World War II, should be included in the discussion of Stalin's terror. This point is not without merit, but the actions against minorities – their forcible displacement to distant regions of the country – were different from the dominant form of terror during the 1930s and it seems best to describe them separately.

The origins of the Great Terror, as the punishment of millions of innocent people came to be called, can be traced in large part to Stalin's determination in mid-1933 to take revenge on members of the Communist Party who had ever held a position on political issues that differed from his. But as was occasionally the case, especially during the early period of the campaign against 'double dealers masked as Bolsheviks', to use Stalin's words of contempt, the General Secretary muddied the waters by also taking some steps that appeared to be conciliatory toward men who had opposed him. For example, in 1928 he ordered the reinstatement in the party of former oppositionists such as

Zinoviev and several others, who then went out of their way to heap praise on Stalin. So did Karl Radek, at one time a supporter of Trotsky, who published an article in *Pravda* on 1 January 1934, entitled 'The Architect of Socialist Society', which gave Stalin credit for having moved the country in a direction that, the writer contended, deserved the approval of all Bolsheviks.

Stalin no doubt was pleased, but he could not overcome his distrust of anyone who had ever opposed him. On 1 June 1933, he ordered a purge from the party of allegedly unreliable people in Moscow, Leningrad, and eight other regions. But these were relatively minor cleansing operations. A startling event, the assassination on 1 December 1934, of Sergei Kirov, the head of the Communist Party in Leningrad, provided him with a pretext for a thorough cleansing of the party, that is, the ousting from the movement of tens of thousands of people he believed were not sufficiently loyal to him.

Stalin had met Kirov in October 1917 and they quickly became close friends even though their personalities were quite different. The friendship extended to the two men's families, who spent vacations together and regularly visited each other's homes. According to the historian Dmitri Volkogonov, who published a biography of Stalin in 1988 based on extensive use of Russian archives, 'there was probably no other party figure for whom Stalin showed such care and even affection, as Kirov.' Unlike Stalin, Kirov was a likable person who attracted a large following within the party. He supported Stalin's policies, but he did not hesitate to speak 'boldly' about major issues without consulting Stalin. He offered mild criticisms of some of the dictator's actions and policies, such as the agrarian program of 1929, but they were so carefully worded that even Stalin did not take offense publicly.

Kirov's assassination was carefully planned and executed by Leonid Nikolaev, a worker who had failed in various menial jobs and had had a checkered career as a member of the Communist Party. He stalked Kirov for several days, and during the afternoon of 1 December he succeeded in locating and shooting him in the Smolny, a series of buildings dating from the eighteenth and nineteenth centuries which after 1918 served as the headquarters of the Communist Party in Leningrad. Kirov was severely wounded and remained alive for only a short time. Guards at the building arrested Nikolaev, who was lying on the floor with a pistol in his hand. He was in some sort of stupor, from which he recovered within three hours.

A day after the assassination, on 2 December, Stalin, accompanied by several leading party officials, arrived in Leningrad to take charge of the investigation. Stalin immediately met Filip Medved, the local chief of the NKVD (secret police), and without saying a word slapped his face to dramatize his dissatisfaction with the officer's failure to protect Kirov. According to an account of Stalin's visit to Leningrad by Nikita Khrushchev, a senior official who rose to the position of General Secretary shortly after Stalin's death in 1953, Nikolaev told Stalin that he had killed Kirov at the behest of an official of the Communist Party. But according to another account of the meeting, Nikolaev told Stalin, 'But you yourself told me—' at which point several secret service policemen hit him and quickly dragged him away. Evidence has come to light that Nikolaev actually told his interrogators that the secret police had planned the assassination and had promised that he would not be punished. In 1937 and 1938, several men involved in planning the assassination were themselves shot. Stalin, it is believed, did not want anyone alive who might give evidence implicating him or his close associates in this sordid affair.

Even now, more than eighty years after the incident, the assassination of Kirov is shrouded in mystery. Several scholars believe that Stalin himself had a hand in planning the murder, and although the evidence is strong, it is not conclusive. Certainly, Stalin had reason to fear Kirov as a rival, and that alone would be enough for the General Secretary to take action against him. In the elections to the Central Committee at the Fifteenth Party

Congress in February 1934, only a handful of delegates (three or four) voted against Kirov, whereas many more (about 123, it is believed) are thought to have cast ballots against Stalin. The exact number is not known because Stalin ordered that all the ballots be destroyed. He also ordered his subordinates to announce that he had received only three negative votes. Moreover, at the same congress, Kirov was greeted with enthusiastic applause, which Stalin apparently interpreted as a sure sign of danger. It was well known that many people had reservations about the inhumane agrarian policies and the government's disregard of democratic procedures in ruling the country. Finally, Kirov had expressed views on foreign policy that differed from Stalin's. Kirov voiced strong dislike for Nazism, a sentiment that may have owed something to the fact that his wife was Jewish. Stalin, however, had indicated early in 1933 that, as Tucker put it, 'he was getting ready to do business with Hitler'.

Within days of the murder, Stalin told some members of his staff that 'to me it is already clear that a well-organized counterrevolutionary terrorist organization is active in Leningrad and that Kirov's murder was its deed. A painstaking investigation must be made.' Even before Stalin made this statement, on the day of Kirov's assassination, the government had issued a decree that ordered the judicial bodies not to 'delay carrying out death sentences involved in crimes' pertaining to the 'planning or carrying out [of] terrorist acts'. Twenty-seven days after the assassination the authorities announced that Nikolaev had belonged to a 'clandestine Trotskyite-Zinovievite terrorist organization' and that he and others implicated in the attack on Kirov had been shot. Andrei Vyshinsky, the Deputy Procurator of the USSR, signed the document and within a few years he would play a critical role in the trials of several senior party members and military officials.

Unexpectedly, in mid-December 1934, the police arrested Zinoviev, Kamenev, and thirteen of their close colleagues on the ground that they had participated in a 'terrorist conspiracy'. All their followers as well as followers of Trotsky were expelled from the Communist Party. These moves marked the beginning of a police crackdown that eventually would affect millions of innocent citizens.

Political trials proved to be the most dramatic action taken by Stalin to crush his opponents, whom he increasingly feared, although, as will become clear, he vastly exaggerated their danger and often manufactured evidence to justify his harsh measures against party members he wanted to eliminate.

Stalin did not invent trials of members of the opposition. In 1922, while Lenin was leader of the country, a political trial had been held, but it was directed at genuine opponents of the communist regime, the Socialist Revolutionaries. Several of their number were charged with having organized an attempt to assassinate Lenin, sponsoring various other terrorist acts, and having collaborated with General A. I. Denikin, a senior officer in the White army that fought against the Bolsheviks during the Civil War. At the trial, the defense was not allowed to question witnesses or to produce documents disproving the charges, rendering a verdict of guilty inevitable. Some of the accused received death sentences, which were eventually suspended, apparently because of extensive criticism of this harsh punishment. The men found guilty were then given long prison sentences.

In 1928, the authorities filed charges against fifty-three engineers in the Donbass on two counts: wrecking equipment and deliberately causing 'accidents' in the workplace. In the judicial proceedings, the so-called Shakhty trial, the evidence brought against the accused was spurious, and scholars now generally acknowledge that the accidents mentioned in the legal charges had resulted not from sabotage but from work by men inexperienced in handling new machinery. Some of the accused confessed, and eleven were sentenced to death, but the government decided to limit that punishment to five of them.

Stalin, however, warned that the incidents in the Donbass indicated that the country faced a serious danger: 'Shakhtyites', he declared, 'are now ensconced in every branch of our industry ... Wrecking by the bourgeois intelligentsia is one of the most dangerous forms of opposition to developing socialism.' Other such proceedings were conducted, but it was only after Kirov's murder that the trials focused on persons who had held prominent positions in the Communist Party or in major institutions such as the army. As will become evident below, these trials involved accused who were innocent of all the charges. But many people in the Soviet Union believed that Stalin had the nation's interests at heart and could not imagine that he would lie about the danger facing the nation. Even some foreign observers of the trials such as Joseph Davies, the United States ambassador to Moscow, were taken in by the testimony. In his autobiography, Davies stated that he had attended sessions of the 'Trial of the Twenty-One', to be discussed below, and was convinced that the defendants were guilty. In a private conversation, he told George Kennan, at that time a senior American official in Moscow, 'They're guilty. I've been a district attorney. I can tell.' In February 1937, Davies sent a letter to President Franklin D. Roosevelt informing him that the trial had demonstrated 'a definite political conspiracy to overthrow the present government'.

Among foreign diplomats in Moscow, Davies represented a tiny minority. Even a superficial examination of the testimony of the defendants reveals that the charges were preposterous. In fact, one of the most bizarre aspects of the trials was the extensive confessions that no one with even a superficial knowledge of modern Russian history or the history of Russian Marxism could have found credible.

The first trial after the murder of Kirov involved Zinoviev and Kamenev and seven of their colleagues. It was conducted in secrecy over a two-day period, on 15–16 January 1935, and, surprisingly, it did not turn out as expected by the authorities.

Andrei Vyshinsky, the prosecutor, wrote a report claiming that the defendants had confessed their guilt in planning the assassination of Kirov. But the prosecutor's failure to provide details suggested that the defendants had not in fact confessed to that crime but had simply acknowledged in general terms that they had 'political culpability' for the assassination. Nevertheless, *Pravda* seized on this information to claim that, 'driven by blind hatred and malice against the party and its leadership, against Comrade Stalin, the genius-continuer of Lenin's cause, the Zinovievist counterrevolutionary gang actively assisted enemies of the Soviet Union to prepare war against her. It trained the fascist mongrels who raised arms against Comrade Kirov.' Compared to later trials, the punishment meted out to Zinoviev and Kamenev was relatively mild: Zinoviev was to be incarcerated for ten years and Kamenev for five.

The outcome did not satisfy Stalin, who longed for a punishment that would permanently remove his perceived enemies and signal to the country that he would not tolerate opposition to his rule. He ordered his legal team to try again. The interrogators improved, or a better word might be 'sharpened', their techniques, and before the second trial, held in August 1936, they persuaded the now sixteen prisoners that it was in their interest to plead guilty to the charges. The prisoners obliged, in large part because officials, including Stalin, and the two lead prosecutors, Genrikh Yagoda and Nikolai Yezhov, had promised that their lives would be spared and their families would not be punished. Whether the prisoners believed these promises is not known, but it is understandable that they would not want to take any chances in their testimony that might provide Stalin and his subordinates with an excuse to mete out the harshest punishment.

It is enlightening to read the confessions that a few of the defendants made to the Supreme Court's Military Collegium, which was charged with hearing the case, because the language they used and the absurdity of the details they revealed are the best indications of the crudeness and politicized character of the entire judicial process. All the defendants, it should be kept in mind, had long been active in left-wing causes, had devoted their lives to Marxist socialism, and had occupied senior positions in the communist movement. Their confessions that they had betrayed their ideals and had become hostile to Lenin's movement were so far-fetched that only the most ardent Stalinists or gullible followers of events in the Soviet Union could have believed them. For example, Zinoviev testified as follows: 'My defective Bolshevism became transformed into anti-Bolshevism and through Trotskyism I arrived at fascism … We filled the place of the Mensheviks, Socialist Revolutionaries and White Guards who could not come out openly in our country.' His colleague and for years closest collaborator, Kamenev, voiced a confession about himself and his co-defendants that was equally bizarre. 'Is it an accident,' he asked the court, 'that alongside of myself [and] Zinoviev … are sitting emissaries of foreign secret police departments, people with false passports, with dubious biographies and undoubted connections with the Gestapo? No! It is not an accident.' These were not the only far-fetched comments by defendants, none of whom could be classified as unintelligent. It may well be that they deliberately made unbelievable statements to alert people to the fact that the entire legal procedure was groundless.

After six days of testimony, Vyshinsky, one of the more passionate Stalinists in the Soviet Union, made the final case for the prosecution. He let loose with a barrage of insults that most people, at least in democracies, would consider inappropriate for a court: 'These mad dogs of capitalism tried to tear limb from limb the best of the best of our Soviet land. They killed one of the men of the revolution who was most dear to us, the admirable and wonderful man, bright and joyous as the smile on his lips was always bright and joyous, as our new life is bright and joyous. They killed our Kirov; they wounded us close to our very heart. They thought they could sow confusion and consternation in our ranks.' He ended his summation with the following appeal: 'I demand that these dogs gone mad should be shot – every one of them.'

The defendants were then allowed to offer their last pleas, and virtually without exception they confessed their guilt and declared that the only just punishment was for them to be shot. Some of the accused condemned themselves as 'dregs' to whom no mercy should be shown. After his short speech of self-incrimination, Kamenev asked permission to address his two sons, one an Air Force pilot and the other still a boy. 'No matter what my sentence will be,' he told his sons, 'I in advance consider it just. Don't look back. Go forward. Together with the Soviet people, follow Stalin.' According to the historian Robert Conquest, 'Others present were shaken, and even the judges are said to have lost their stony expression.' Interestingly, when one of the defendants, G. E. Evdokimov, made his confession, he blurted out, apparently unintentionally, a few words that must have distressed the prosecutors: 'Who will believe a single word of ours?'

The trial lasted six days and after deliberating for seven hours the judges pronounced all the defendants guilty and condemned them to death. That the charges were fabricated became evident beyond doubt some time later when readers of the testimony discovered that the NKVD had accused one of the defendants of having received orders from Trotsky in 1932 at the Hotel Bristol in Copenhagen to hamper the growth of the Soviet economy and also to arrange a plot against Stalin. That hotel, it turned out, had been razed fifteen years earlier. By the time this evidence came to light, the accused had been shot – the secret police took care of that hours after the verdict.

Within a few months of this trial, in January 1937, another prosecution was under way, this one against Karl Radek, Yuri Pyatakov, and fifteen other former senior Bolsheviks. All were accused of having discussed plans with Trotsky to remove Stalin from power, and during the trial they all provided details of their machinations. Stalin was especially eager to secure Radek's confession; he visited him at the Lubyanka prison and in the presence of Yezhov promised Radek that he would not face the death sentence if he confessed. Radek obliged by manufacturing a vast amount of information on the plot to kill Stalin. He is generally regarded as having provided the prosecution with the most detailed, albeit manufactured, scenario of the plotters' intentions. Other defendants followed suit and soon the prosecutors had more than enough information to proceed with the trial. When it was his turn to testify, Radek gave testimony that the historian Conquest has described as a 'brilliant showing ... While the other accused spoke flatly and drearily, he put feeling into his evidence.' On 30 January 1937, the judges announced that all were guilty and all except Radek and two others were sentenced to death. But many years later, scholars discovered that on 19 May 1939, Radek was killed in jail. To date, no details on the circumstances surrounding his death have surfaced.

In 1938, another show trial took place in Moscow over a twelve-day period, 2–13 March, and it is often referred to as the 'greatest trial of all', the Trial of the Twenty-One. Bukharin, one of Lenin's favorites, was the most eminent Old Bolshevik in the dock, but the trial became especially famous because it included Genrikh Yagoda, head of the NKVD until 1937 when, according to the editors of the 1964 edition of Lenin's works, he was 'expelled from the Party for systematic breaches of socialist legality'. Stalin probably wanted to be rid of him because he knew too much about the decisions made at the highest level of the regime. But there are other possible reasons for Stalin's interest in being rid of Yagoda. He was widely believed to have been involved in planning Kirov's murder. Also, Stalin may have tired of him because he had at one time been close to some of the rightists within Bolshevism. Moreover, Yagoda was a Jew and at this time Stalin was again trying to curry favor with Hitler by reducing the influence of Jews in the Soviet political hierarchy. Finally, it has been speculated that Stalin may have wanted the blame for many of the crimes carried out at the dictator's orders to be shifted to Yagoda.

Once the trial began, there were the usual confessions, but to everyone's surprise, a fair number of the accused refused to cave in to the questions of the President of the Court, V. V. Ulrikh, a judge who had presided at many of the political trials. Nikolai Krestinsky, formerly a deputy foreign commissar, was the first to refuse to give the expected answers. He acknowledged that he had made a confession in the preliminary investigation but now declared: 'I am not guilty. I am not a Trotskyite, I was never a member of the bloc of Rights and Trotskyites, of whose existence I was not aware. Nor have I committed any of the crimes with which I personally am charged, in particular I plead not guilty to the charge of having had connections with the German intelligence service.' When Vyshinsky took over the questioning and pressed him to admit his guilt, Krestinsky still refused to do so. But one day later, he retracted and pleaded guilty; it is still not clear why he changed his mind.

Bukharin sparred with Vyshinsky and at first failed to give straight answers. He acknowledged having been 'one of the outstanding leaders of this "bloc of Rights and Trotskyites". Consequently, I plead guilty to what directly follows from this, the sum total of crimes committed by this counterrevolutionary organization, irrespective of whether or not I knew of, whether or not I took a direct part in any particular act.' But in response to several other questions about the crimes, Bukharin consistently denied knowledge of espionage by his colleagues. And to a direct question by Vyshinsky as to whether he would plead guilty to espionage, Bukharin answered: 'I do not.' He continued in this vein, but the prosecutor remained adamant. It may be that Bukharin finally decided to be more forthright in his answers because he had concluded some time earlier that he would not survive long under the Stalinist regime. Eighteen months before his trial, while he was on a mission in Western Europe, he told several Mensheviks that Stalin 'will finish us all off ... He's Satan ... We are all doomed.'

The judges left the courtroom at 9:25 P.M. on 12 March and returned with a verdict eighteen hours and thirty-five minutes later. All were found guilty and all except three were sentenced to death. But in 1941 one of the three was resentenced and shot; the other two were also shot, apparently without having been formally resentenced.

ANDREI VYSHINSKY (1883–1954)

Next to Stalin, Vyshinsky was probably the most despised Soviet official. Historian Robert Conquest met him during his final year of service, when he held the post of Foreign Secretary, and concluded that he was 'both physically and spiritually a creature who gave life to the worn image of a "rat in human form".' It was generally believed that one reason he became a flunky of Stalin was his fear that some party leaders would expose his unforgivable initial political commitment: until 1920 he had been a Menshevik, and to communists that meant that he had betrayed Marxism, an unpardonable sin.

Stalin no doubt sensed Vyshinsky's insecurity and that was probably why he appointed him to senior posts in the government – the dictator wanted persons in office who could be relied upon to carry out his most ruthless orders without hesitation. In 1936, he appointed him Procurator-General of the USSR and Vyshinsky's role was to question leading officials whom Stalin wanted to liquidate. Vyshinsky loyally carried out the dictator's wishes, but as the historian V. G. Trukhanevsky pointed out in 1994, the procurator paid a heavy price for acting as Stalin's henchman: 'Vyshinsky was terrified of Stalin. Every Thursday he would go and report to him, and well beforehand, in anticipation of the encounter his mood would sour. The closer it came to Thursday, the gloomier and more irritable he got ... But by Friday, when it was all behind him, he allowed himself to relax for a day or two. Experienced people knew that this was when it was best to report to him on the most complicated matters or approach him with requests of a personal nature.' Stalin, the historian continued, 'was a merciless boss'.

In 1940, Vyshinsky became Deputy Minister and in 1949 he moved to the top spot of the Foreign Ministry, and he again followed Stalin's orders, delivering savage attacks on the United States in the United Nations. He died in 1954, one year after Stalin's death.

In some respects the most dramatic trial – and certainly the most harmful to the Soviet Union because it involved men responsible for the defense of the country, now presumed to be under threat from the capitalist world – began on 11 June 1937. At 9 A.M. that day, Marshal M. N. Tukhachevsky, a soldier widely regarded as an unusually gifted officer who had made outstanding contributions to the communist cause during the Civil War as a strategist and theorist, was in the dock, together with eight other generals, charged with having been part of a 'foul counterrevolutionary military-Fascist organization', which had intended to assassinate leaders of the Soviet Communist Party and the Soviet state and then seize power with the help of Nazi Germany. In addition to his senior military post, Tukhachevsky had been a member of the Central Committee of the Communist Party, from which he had been expelled on 26 May. Moreover, he had been arrested only two weeks before the trial began, which means that the interrogation was conducted with extraordinary speed. Stalin played a central role in the preparations for the trial. He met twice with Vyshinsky, the prosecutor, and shortly before the trial began, with Ulrikh, the presiding judge, to give them instructions on the conduct of the case.

Both the marshal and the other defendants had been tortured and as a result agreed to admit guilt, which, however, they did rather listlessly. The trial was closed and short: it began at 9 A.M. and ended before lunchtime the same day. A couple of hours later, the judges announced that all were guilty and would be shot. According to an account by Khrushchev, then a senior official in the government, 'when [Army Commander I. E.] Yakir was shot he exclaimed: "Long live the Party, long live Stalin!" ... When Stalin was told how Yakir had behaved before his death, he cursed Yakir.' The families of the executed officers were also punished, by banishment to Astrakhan, a city in southern European Russia, about nine hundred miles from Moscow.

MARSHAL M. N. TUKHACHEVSKY (1893–1937)

The fate of Marshal M. N. Tukhachevsky in June 1937 is emblematic of the malignant political system of the Soviet Union in the 1930s. As a young man, he joined the Russian army at the beginning of World War I, and fought bravely until his capture by the Germans in 1917; released later that year, he returned to Russia and joined the Bolshevik party. He served the revolutionary cause faithfully during the Civil War (1918–20) and impressed his superiors. During the 1920s he rapidly rose to a senior position in the Red Army and, like most of his comrades, he believed that Stalin was the legitimate ruler of the country, and was proud to serve the new order. He stood out as a brilliant organizer and strategist and many considered him to be the smartest man in the Soviet military services. By the time he was in his early forties, he occupied the prestigious position of Deputy People's Commissar of Defense.

But a paranoid Stalin convinced himself that senior officers were planning to overthrow his government. On 11 June 1937, several newspapers carried an announcement that stunned readers: the marshal and several other officers in the Red Army had confessed to 'a breach of military duty and of the oath of allegiance, treason to their country, treason against the peoples of the USSR and treason against the Workers' and Peasants' Red Army'. The following day, the authorities released a second statement: the officers had already been tried and all of them had been executed. Stalin, it is now known, had given Andrei Vyshinsky, the lead prosecutor of the trial, final instructions on how to conduct the trial and on the 'appropriate' punishments.

Scholars have found no evidence to substantiate the charges against the marshal. The archive of the Nazi regime in Germany, with whom Tukhachevsky was said to have plotted, yielded no evidence of contact between German officials and senior Soviet officers. And in 1957, four years after Stalin's death, the Soviet Supreme Court formally cleared Tukhachevsky and his colleagues of all charges and consequently their membership in the Communist Party was restored.

Many people in the 1930s found the spectacle of the trials puzzling and they continue to puzzle some people even today. Why would leading members of the Communist Party, participants in the struggles against the tsarist regime as well as in establishing the Bolshevik system of rule after the Revolution of 1917, betray the cause to which they had dedicated their lives? Why would they confess to having taken part in a conspiracy to wreck the Soviet economy, to overthrow Stalin, to plot together with Fascists, avowed enemies of Marxism? The novelist Arthur Koestler offered one explanation that received widespread approval in his gripping book *Darkness at Noon*: that the accused were such staunch party members that they offered confessions as a last service to a noble cause. They feared that if they publicly defended themselves and accused Stalin and his henchmen of murdering loyal communists, they would split the Marxist movement and endanger the socialist state. A similar explanation may be given for Trotsky's statement quoted above, that the party was always right no matter what decisions it took.

Another explanation for the defendants' abject behavior may be more persuasive: that they had been beaten down by their isolation in dingy prison cells. Many had been subjected to horrendous physical torture; often they had also been promised that they would be spared the death sentence. Some were warned that their families would be harmed if they did not plead guilty as charged. In the vast majority of cases, the NKVD, under instructions from Stalin, did not honor these promises. A large percentage of the accused were executed and in many cases their families were subjected to various punishments.

It should also be kept in mind that all in all only seventy persons were cajoled into making pubic confessions; the vast majority of those who were executed were never subjected to a trial, certainly not one open to visitors. To obtain and publicize confessions was a clever public relations ploy that convinced a fair number among the Soviet populace that those on trial were guilty, and, as already noted, even in Western countries some people believed that the charges leveled at senior communists had merit. But it is also noteworthy that Stalin permitted only a very small number of accused to voice public denials of guilt, no doubt because he feared that ordinary citizens might prove less malleable than the most senior party officials.

Given the rise to power of Hitler in Germany in 1933 and the threat he posed to the Soviet Union, no Soviet institution should have been considered more sacrosanct than the military. But instead of strengthening the Soviet military forces, Stalin conducted a purge that weakened them significantly and unnecessarily. In a circular he drafted for the armed forces, he demanded that his officials purge not only outspoken enemies of his government but also the 'silent ones', that is, those who failed to report 'enemies of the people'. Within a matter of months, Stalin ordered the arrest and in many cases the execution of 3 of 5 marshals, 13 of 15 army commanders, 220 of 406 brigade commanders, 57 of 85 corps commanders, 110 of 195 division commanders, all 11 commissars of war, 75 of 80 members of the Supreme Military Council, ninety percent of all generals, and eighty percent of all colonels. All told, between twenty and thirty percent of all officers were purged. Traditional dictators would never have decapitated their army in this way because their political power depended to a considerable degree on the support of the military establishment. Totalitarian leaders, however, had other sources of power: most notably a strong police force, party loyalists, and personal charisma.

Although Stalin did not invent state terrorism in the Soviet Union, he vastly enlarged its scope. Prior to 1934, the government sought to root out people believed to be engaged in activities designed to undermine the new order; from 1934 to 1937, the government targeted 'former oppositionists' and those believed to be disloyal to Stalin; after 1937, as Adam Ulam pointed out, terror 'became an everyday feature of life, a reflection of its maker's belief that this was the most efficacious and economical way of ruling the country, and that nobody ... should be beyond its reach'. A trivial remark such as that 'the material situation of workers is getting worse' was enough to lead to imprisonment.

No area of the country, no ethnic group, and not even Stalin's relatives escaped the Great Terror. In 1937, the police arrested S. S. Redens, who was married to Anna Alliluyeva, the sister of Stalin's former wife who had committed suicide. Redens's father-in-law, a committed Bolshevik, never asked Stalin, his relative by marriage, what had happened to his son-in-law, whose wife, Anna, was shattered by the disappearance of her husband. Svetlana thought that Anna's father 'had too much pride to ask for anything'. It may also be that he was afraid to ask, or perhaps he was such a committed Bolshevik that he did not consider it appropriate to question Stalin on so sensitive a matter. Another one of Stalin's relatives, Alexander Semyonovich Svadnidze, the brother of Stalin's first wife, was arrested in 1937 and shot in 1941. Apparently, Stalin distrusted him because he was an Old Bolshevik who harbored some heretical views, even though he had at one time been Stalin's friend. The official reason for executing him was that he had served as an agent of German intelligence officials, a charge that hardly seems credible. The list of Stalin's relatives who became victims of the purges is longer than indicated here, but the point has been made that the dictator was indiscriminate in his determination to eliminate all those suspected of opposing him, however dubious the evidence. As far as Stalin was concerned, no one was above suspicion, and his senior officials were fully aware of that.

In his biography of Nikita S. Khrushchev, William Taubman relates the following comment made by Nikolai Bulganin to Khrushchev, both of whom had served as close advisers to the dictator, as they were driving home from Stalin's dacha: 'Sometimes when you go to Stalin's, he invites you as a friend. But while you're sitting with him, you don't know where they'll take you afterward: home or to prison.' In his famous speech to the Twentieth Congress, which will be discussed in more detail below, Khrushchev leveled an even more damaging charge against the dictator: that he planned to eliminate all his closest political associates.

Even the most senior officials did not dare question Stalin's decisions to punish their closest relatives. In 1949, Stalin ordered that Polina Molotov be exiled to Siberia for five years. Polina was the Jewish wife of Vyacheslav Molotov, the Foreign Minister and for many years a member of Stalin's inner circle. She was found guilty of various trumped-up charges, among them that she had expressed support for the newly established state of Israel. As far as is known, her husband never protested or even raised the subject with Stalin. Was he motivated by fear or by unwillingness to speak out against the man who, he may have believed, had transformed Russia into a vastly improved society and whose conduct could therefore not be questioned? It remains a riddle.

Stalin's purges, it should be kept in mind, were not restricted to senior officials and prominent citizens. He was determined to change the composition of the party by bringing in new recruits who were 'simple people'. During the eight-month period between May and December 1935, about 190,000 party members were expelled. The process continued, and it is estimated that by the beginning of 1939, some 850,000 had been ousted from the party.

But many more citizens were arrested on flimsy charges of hostility to the authorities and sent to labor camps. Conditions there were miserable. Stalin's principal objective was to terrorize the population, and force them to accept orders from the authorities in Moscow, a goal the dictator achieved. When Stalin heard complaints about conditions in the camps, he dismissed them as 'demagogical and unfounded'. The great writer A. L. Solzhenitsyn provides a harrowing account of his 8 years in the Gulag and its history and administration in his books, *The Gulag Archipelago, One day in the life of Ivan Denisovich,* and *The First Circle.*

LABOR CAMPS (GULAG)

In the *Times Literary Supplement* of 4 December 2015, the historian David Motadel pointed out that labor camps, or concentration camps, 'were part of the machinery of mass oppression designed not only to isolate, punish and silence those incarcerated, but also, more generally, to strengthen political domination and social control. Often organized without modern bureaucratic structures and ruled with sophisticated methods of discipline and terror, the camps subjected prisoners to slave labor, torture, malnutrition and other forms of physical violence.' Such camps made their first appearance in Bolshevik Russia in 1918 and came to be known as the Gulag, an abbreviation for the government agency that administered them from 1929.

By the late 1930s, the authorities in Moscow had developed a vast system of close to five hundred camps and labor colonies. By 1953 an estimated fourteen million people had served time in the camps. It is thought one half of the inmates were there for alleged political crimes, such as voicing discontent with the government, but many were incarcerated arbitrarily and without trial. Other prisoners had no idea why they had been arrested, and a fair number of committed Bolsheviks who had been sent to the camps were convinced that a mistake had been made and that they would soon be freed.

Conditions at the camps were horrendous; inmates were forced to spend ten to twelve hours a day working in mines or forests. Their rations were minimal, about five hundred grams of bread or gruel a day with small amounts of liquids. Some eight hundred thousand to nine hundred thousand are estimated to have been executed, and anywhere between 1.6 million to 10 million people died there. After Stalin's death in 1953, his successors began to dismantle the camps.

Importantly, Stalin was not simply a dictator who gave general orders to his subordinates to carry out what might be called the 'terror from above'. There is ample evidence, some of which has already been touched upon, that he played a critical role in implementing the terror. He instructed his officials on exactly who was to be incarcerated and who was to be shot, and at times he visited former party leaders and assured them that if they cooperated with the secret police and made detailed confessions they would not be executed, assurances that he intended to ignore. On occasion, Stalin sat in a room next to the courtroom and through a hole in the wall watched the interrogations of political prisoners to make certain that the prosecutors and judges carried out his orders. He carefully examined the interrogators' reports, and when Kamenev seemed reluctant to talk, Stalin demanded that the interrogators demonstrate their effectiveness. 'Don't come to me,' he told them, 'without Kamenev's confession.' The officials knew enough about Stalin's mode of governing to understand that failure on their part could be costly to their careers and their lives.

Frequently, Stalin, together with one of his senior officials, would study lists of people who were being proposed for execution. Among the documents discovered in Russian archives, lists have been found that include 230,000 names, all of them under consideration for severe punishment. On a single day, 12 December 1938, Stalin and Molotov approved the shooting of 3,167 people, whose names appeared on various sheets of paper. After the two men signed these papers, they went to see a film, Stalin's favorite pastime. On another occasion, Yezhov had sent Stalin a list of people who were about to be tried by a military court on the charge of having committed capital crimes. Stalin placed a brief message on the list: 'Shoot all 138 of them.' And still another time, when he was asked to comment on a proposal by Yezhov to execute 208 men and 15 women accused of being 'enemies of the people' and two hundred soldiers suspected of the same crime, Stalin simply wrote, 'In favor'.

A major consequence of the terror was the loss of experienced employees in important positions by the Communist Party, the government, and industry. For younger people, this loss created an opening for jobs that they did not expect to be available for many years, and they were bound to be grateful to Stalin.

Although Stalin was the chief architect of the economic and social changes in the Soviet Union, he had to rely on subordinates to carry out his wishes. He made sure to choose people he could depend on not only to follow his orders in every detail but also to do so with so much enthusiasm that they would siphon off blame that might be heaped on the dictator himself. He was especially concerned to place the right persons as heads of the NKVD, a police organization charged with rooting out people suspected of a lack of enthusiasm for communism by bringing charges against them in rigged courts or arbitrarily dispatching them to labor camps (the Gulag). Stalin evinced no compunction about resorting to the most brutal methods to achieve his goals, but he wanted the Soviet public as well as people abroad to believe that the men and women executed or imprisoned were in fact guilty.

N. I. YEZHOV (1895–1940)

The career of Nikolai I. Yezhov illustrates some of the more bizarre and brutal aspects of Stalin's dictatorship. Yezhov joined the Leninist movement in May 1917 and rose rapidly to a high position in the Communist Party. In 1934, he became a member of the Central Committee of the party and in 1936 he was appointed head of the People's Commissariat of Internal Affairs (NKVD). In selecting Yezhov, Stalin chose a man ideally suited for this nefarious assignment. Boris Nicolaevsky, a Menshevik activist, wrote that in 'the whole of my life, I have never met a more repellent personality than Yezhov's. When I look at him I am reminded irresistibly of the wicked urchins of the courts in Rasterayeva Street, whose favorite occupation was to tie a piece of paper dipped in kerosene to a cat's tail, set fire to it, and then watch with delight how the terrified animal would tear down the street, trying desperately but in vain to escape the approaching flames.'

But when Stalin concluded late in 1938 that the repression of millions of innocent citizens was weakening the country and therefore needed to be relaxed, he picked Yezhov as the man to serve as the scapegoat for the brutalities inflicted upon so many people. In November 1938 Yezhov, seeing the handwriting on the wall, asked to be relieved as the People's Commissar for Internal Affairs, but this did not satisfy Stalin. Within a few months Yezhov was charged with membership of a group that plotted to persuade Stalin's bodyguard to murder the country's leader. Documents made available after the collapse of the Soviet Union in 1991 reveal that Yezhov claimed that he himself had exposed the plot. Stalin rejected the confession with the claim that Yezhov was lying so that he could avoid punishment. In April 1939, he confessed that he was indeed part of the plot and for good measure he named 150 other officials as accomplices. Yezhov and all his alleged accomplices were shot without the benefit of a trial. Stalin's attempt to absolve himself for the terror of the 1930s may have succeeded in persuading some of his contemporaries of his innocence, but few historians in the West and a growing number in contemporary Russia remain unconvinced.

The arrests of citizens were often based on little more than denunciations by neighbors or acquaintances, a practice highly praised by the NKVD, so much so that even children who exposed the misdeeds of their parents were glorified. Early in the 1930s, Pavel Morozov, a fourteen-year-old who lived in a Urals village, denounced his father for keeping property that he had confiscated from kulaks and for 'hoarding' grain that did not belong to him. The father was tried, found guilty, and executed. The enraged villagers took revenge upon the boy by killing him.

But the government honored the boy by naming him a major 'Pioneer hero' (the Pioneers were a youth organization similar to Western Scouts), and he was prominently listed in the Pioneer 'Book of Heroism'. His name was also attached to the Palace of Culture of Young Pioneers in Moscow, even though it was later discovered that Stalin did not admire him for denouncing his father; he actually called him a 'little swine'. But he nevertheless approved of the boy's glorification because it was politically helpful in the campaign to break the resistance of peasants opposed to collectivization.

In his choice of heads of the NKVD, Stalin succeeded in finding men who thrived on work that many people would shun. All three, Genrikh Yagoda from 1934 to 1936, Nikolai Yezhov from 1936 to 1938, and Lavrenti Beria from 1938 to 1945, were ruthless and sadistic, but by all accounts Beria was the most vicious. Svetlana, Stalin's daughter, put much of the blame for the terror on Beria: 'My father was astonishingly helpless before Beria's machinations. All Beria had to do was bring him the record of the interrogation in which X "confessed", or others "confessed" for him or, worse yet, X refused to "confess".' She also claimed that Beria's 'influence on my father grew and grew and never ceased until the day of my father's death'. This account of Stalin's role in the terror is misleading, as the previous description of his involvement in the trials and purges has shown, and at one point Svetlana herself conceded that the two 'were guilty together'. But it is true that Beria outdid his two predecessors in sadism. He had made his start in politics in Georgia, as did Stalin, and they had worked together for some years. In 1934, Beria supervised the establishment of Stalin's Institute, which featured material designed to demonstrate that Stalin had played a critical role in the creation and success of the Bolshevik movement. Stalin knew what kind of person he was putting in charge of the political police.

Beria enjoyed inflicting torture on prisoners, and he made it a practice on most evenings to visit one of his offices in a Moscow prison; he insisted on having his own office in every prison in the capital so that he could personally supervise the interrogation of inmates who had been tortured. Every morning he would call a meeting of the Military Collegium to announce the punishment of the prisoners he had seen the night before. Beria also was reputed to enjoy forced sex with women picked up by his drivers. Even some of his colleagues found Beria unbearable. After Stalin's death in 1953, he began to lord it over some fellow members of a small group of senior advisers to Stalin who feared that he was seeking to take over the leadership of the government. In 1953, Khrushchev, by then First Secretary of the Central Committee, ordered the arrest and trial of Beria on charges of treason and various other crimes. The other members of the Bolshevik leadership agreed with Khrushchev's decision. Beria was found guilty and quickly executed. It was not exactly an impressive show of support for the rule of law, but it did indicate revulsion at the despicable behavior by Beria over many years. Beria's predecessors, Yagoda and Yezhov, had been executed while Stalin was still alive, most probably because the dictator wanted them to be viewed as responsible for the terror. The dismissal of Yezhov late in 1938 is still something of a mystery. He was an alcoholic and Stalin may have suspected him of plotting against him. It is known that Yezhov was shot, but we do not know exactly when. His dismissal marked the end of *Yezhovshchina*, the name given to the most violent period of the terror.

GENRIKH YAGODA, 1891–1938

Genrikh Yagoda was yet another leader of the NKVD (Commissariat of Internal Affairs) to discover the hazards of occupying a senior position in Stalin's government. Given their character, none of those men should have been surprised. As Adam Ulam pointed out, the three most prominent men who led the NKVD in the 1930s were 'monstrous, each in a different way'. Yagoda 'was a hardened scoundrel and intriguer who grew up with the GPU and whom Stalin never trusted'.

Yagoda achieved much that should have pleased Stalin: he organized the first so-called 'show trial' in Moscow that resulted in the shooting of two long-standing leaders of Bolshevism, Grigory Zinoviev and Lev Kamenev, both of whom were condemned to death for allegedly having planned to assassinate the Soviet leader; he brought charges of disloyalty to Stalin against several senior army officers; and he greatly increased the number of slave laborers, whose work was important for the Soviet economy. But Stalin considered these achievements inadequate. On 15 September 1936, he sent a telegram to several members of the Politburo in which he contended that Yagoda had 'definitely proved himself incapable of unmasking the Trotskyite–Zinoviev bloc', which was supposedly plotting to take power. Few in the party hierarchy believed that Yagoda was dismissed for incompetence. Many party officials agreed that Stalin had turned against Yagoda because he had serious doubts about his political reliability. Two years after his dismissal, Yagoda was tried for spying for Germany as well as on other, somewhat lesser charges. Found guilty, he was shot, not the only head of the NKVD to meet this fate.

Why was there no organized resistance to the terror that affected so many millions of Soviet citizens? It is an intriguing question that cannot be ignored or easily answered. Likely, the most important reason is that many people saw in Stalin a godlike figure, a wise man with a better understanding than anyone else of how the country should be ruled. The notion that the leader of Russia, until 1917 the Tsar, was the all-knowing father who cared about the well-being of his people, was a deep-seated conviction among the masses, and even today that notion persists among many people in the Russian Federation.

In addition, Stalin was a clever politician who took care not to antagonize too many sectors of the population at any one time. For example, when he launched the campaign against the kulaks in 1929, and when he purged the police in 1938, he relaxed tensions within the Communist Party, reducing the risk that opposition to him might emerge that might be too extensive for him to crush.

One should recall, however, that to a large extent the purges affected people who had been loyal to the regime and remained loyal to the Bolshevik cause. Not surprisingly, many of them could not fathom why they were being punished. They felt certain that they were innocent of wrongdoing and assumed that they would soon be released from jail or the labor camps. Their view of how to react to the terror can be summarized as 'Better lie low and hope for the best'. Also, a sizable number of the people victimized by the terror had been so deeply influenced by the government's propaganda that they believed that while they themselves were innocent, other prisoners were surely guilty of anti-government activities. They persuaded themselves that their arrest was an unfortunate accident that could not be avoided in a historical process that might be unfair to some people but necessary for the good of the cause. Finally, a large number of victims concluded that the Stalinist regime was so firmly entrenched that opposition to it was pointless.

Various explanations have been offered for the wholesale slaughter and imprisonment of masses of people, but the blood-letting was so capricious and harmful that ultimately none seems entirely convincing, and the search for an answer to this question continues. The decrees on the purges, recently made public, claimed that they were directed to a large extent at categories of people who were suspected of harboring strong anti-Bolshevik views, such as former kulaks, ethnic minorities, and those who at one time had supported political parties hostile to communism. But this contention is not conclusive. As already noted, many of the victims had in fact been loyal members of the Communist Party and many others had never expressed views hostile to the authorities.

Some scholars have suggested that Stalin ordered the trials of former political leaders as well as the purges of the Communist Party because they enabled him to divert attention from the failings of the Five Year Plans and the hardships endured by the masses. Another explanation stresses Stalin's determination to root out all possibility of opposition to his dictatorial power, which, given all the evidence of his brutality, seems to be the most plausible explanation. Several specialists on the history of the Soviet Union have concluded that a person with Stalin's penchant for violence should be considered a monster, which is not an inaccurate term for the man who ruled the Soviet Union from 1929 to 1953.

This interpretation is consistent with one put forth some sixty years ago by Merle Fainsod, a foremost scholar of the Soviet Union: 'The insecurity of the masses must be supplemented by the insecurity of the governing elite, who surround the Supreme Dictator.' No official could be allowed to build up a strong following lest he become strong enough to challenge Stalin. Under the repressive Stalinist regime any citizen might well have good reason to be disloyal, and thus the leader and his regime could be completely secure 'only if everyone is sufficiently terrorized to become incapable of acting independently'.

In 1938, the authorities took steps to reduce significantly the state's terror against its own people, probably because Stalin realized that if he continued on the path of violence the entire system might collapse. Some evidence suggests that party members had become so fearful of the terror that a fair number in low-level work refused to move into a position of authority that would be more likely to expose them to police scrutiny. Whatever the reason, in April 1938 the Central Committee plenum put out a warning against 'exaggerated vigilance' and placed the blame for the 'excesses' of the preceding five years on local party committees, 'traitors', and Trotskyites who 'had wormed their way into the security organs'. But Stalin did not repudiate the terror, nor did he strip the secret police of its authority to maintain a watchful eye on citizens who might be critical of his rule.

In fact, the most notorious act of violence in this relatively calm period took place in August 1940, and was directed at Leon Trotsky, the man who had been Stalin's chief rival for leadership of the Soviet Union in the 1920s. It is hard to explain Stalin's endless obsession with Trotsky, who had left the Soviet Union in 1929 and was now living in the countryside near Mexico City. True, Trotsky continued to write about current affairs, he still commented extensively on developments in the Soviet Union, and he invariably and sharply criticized Stalin's policies whenever he had the chance. But his following was not large and his influence in his homeland, as far as can be determined, was negligible. Some historians believe that the best explanation for Stalin's pursuit of his competitor for the mantle of Lenin's legacy is that the Soviet ruler was psychologically incapable of tolerating anyone who had ever challenged him, especially if that person still carried some weight in the world of Marxism. Others contend that in 1939 Stalin feared an outbreak of war and therefore considered it necessary to eliminate Trotsky lest he provide aid to the Soviet Union's enemies.

Whatever the reason, in August 1940 a Spanish communist under orders from the Soviet secret police gained entrance to Trotsky's study and hacked at his skull with an axe, killing him almost instantly. In Mexico, the murderer received a twenty-year prison sentence, but in Moscow Stalin bestowed an honor on him *in absentia*.

7

Was the Stalinist State Totalitarian?

Stalin's ambition, as already suggested, was not simply to dominate Soviet politics. He also considered himself an expert on culture defined in the broadest terms, and he was determined to recast it, to bring it in line with his understanding of Marxism. Stalin had indicated as early as the summer of 1930, at the Sixteenth Party Congress, that he was thinking of radical changes in Soviet culture. He declared that it should become 'national in form and socialist in content'. Six years later, Stalin elaborated on this slogan: the culture of all the nationalities that constituted the Soviet Union should be consistent with the principles of the Communist Party, although writers and artists should express their works in local languages. It soon became clear that every writer and scholar would be expected to toe the new line.

The press and other media claimed that since Stalin was a 'genius', his judgements must be the final word on all subjects. Most intellectuals bowed to his will, just as political leaders did when they realized that they had been defeated by his machinations. Some historians have referred to this development as a 'cultural revolution from above'. Nadezhda Mandelshtam, the wife of the distinguished poet and essayist Osip Mandelshtam, who refused to cave in to Stalin's directive on culture, coined another term for Stalin's campaign to dominate Soviet culture; she called it a 'conspiracy from above'.

A few examples will suffice to indicate the scope of this 'revolution' or 'conspiracy'. Officials loyal to Stalin controlled the daily press and publishing houses and consequently they did not print anything at all seriously critical of the men in power. Government officials also screened all textbooks used in schools and universities. The study of Marxism as interpreted by the authorities in Moscow was obligatory in all academic institutions.

Government officials and censors paid special attention to the work of historians because of Stalin's ambition to have the Soviet people understand the past as he did. For example, the historian M. N. Pokrovsky, a committed Marxist, a supporter of Bolshevism, and probably the most highly praised historian in the 1920s, came under severe criticism for not mentioning the 'just wars' that the country had waged in the past. In general, Stalin and his supporters wanted historians to return to such subjects as famous battles, especially those that Russia had won, and to put more emphasis on famous kings and dates, subjects that most Marxists tended to play down in favor of detailed descriptions of class struggles. Scholars who agreed with Pokrovsky's approach to history were denounced as 'enemies of the people' and quite a few of them became victims of the Stalinist terror.

The overarching principle to guide writers in the humanities and especially in literature was the doctrine of 'socialist realism'. Writers were obliged to portray life in the Soviet Union as defined by the Communist Party and were expected to depict a brighter future that would result from the continuing implementation of socialist ideals. In short, authors had to focus on what life would be like in the future, when all citizens would be guaranteed decent living conditions. As Stalin put it, novelists living under Bolshevism must serve as 'engineers of human souls'. Put differently, their primary task was to imbue the people with the ideals of the Communist Party.

Stalin also took it upon himself to censor plays and movies. There are many examples of his tampering with productions in these fields, but one will suffice to give the reader an idea of how Stalin's mind operated in this cultural area. In 1944, Sergei Eisenstein, an outstanding film director, produced a movie on Tsar Ivan IV, also known as Ivan the Terrible because he had governed the country in the years from 1547 to 1584 with extreme cruelty. Ivan made extensive use of the *Oprichnina*, a police force that dealt brutally with anyone who dared to oppose him. But he also won many battles against foreigners and had succeeded in enlarging what was then Russia.

In the first part of a projected trilogy on Ivan, Eisenstein avoided the unsavory aspects of the Tsar's reign. Highly praised, the film was awarded the Stalin Prize, a great honor. But in the second film Eisenstein depicted the seamier aspects of Ivan's rule, which infuriated Stalin. He was a strong admirer of the Tsar, no doubt because he saw the sixteenth-century ruler as a model for himself. In fact, in a history textbook published in 1937 that Stalin admired, Tsar Ivan IV appears as a great hero. A key sentence in the book reads as follows: 'Under the reign of Ivan IV Russia's possessions were greatly enlarged. His kingdom became one of the biggest states in the world.' That achievement, according to the author, was possible only because the ruler had crushed the treasonous *boyars* (nobles).

Stalin reminded Eisenstein of Ivan's achievements, and insisted that the Tsar was a 'great and wise ruler' whose military forces constituted a 'progressive army'. Stalin granted that 'Ivan the Terrible was very ruthless ... One can show that he was ruthless. But you must show why it was necessary to be ruthless.' Obviously, Stalin viewed himself as a ruler in the mold of Ivan IV. True, he was ruthless, but necessarily so for the well-being of Russia. The government did not permit the showing of Eisenstein's film; it was kept in the closet until 1957, four years after Stalin's death.

In the sciences, the most notable example of government interference was the case of the agronomist T. D. Lysenko, who put forth a theory that no respectable scientist in the West and few in Russia could accept. Initially, he had argued that if farmers treated wheat seeds with liquid and then kept them in a cold container, they could be planted in the spring to produce a crop in the summer. This was welcome news in the Soviet Union because it meant that farmers could avoid the harm to crops caused by the winter cold in such areas as the Ukraine. Farmers achieved some successes by following Lysenko's advice, but then the agronomist made a further claim for the process he had invented that immediately raised eyebrows in the scientific community not only in the West but also in the Soviet Union. Lysenko asserted that plants would inherit the vernalized state and consequently would no longer require the process he had invented. This amounted to a claim that acquired characteristics were inheritable, a notion that harked back to the pre-Darwinian era and that had long been dismissed by scholars. Soon after Stalin's death, even the Soviet authorities no longer gave it credence. Lysenkism, as it was called, was then generally considered an example of an attempt by politicians to interfere, unwisely, in a field that was beyond their ken.

Stalin's single most influential contribution to Soviet culture was the publication in 1938 of the *History of the Communist Party of the Soviet Union (Bolsheviks): Short Course*, which quickly became required reading for anyone who hoped to succeed at school or in any profession. In its announcement on 15 November 1938 of the availability of the book, *Pravda* indicated that the *Short Course*, as it soon came to be known, would be the basic text on Soviet politics. Because it was written in simple language – many paragraphs consist of one sentence – the general public could easily understand its contents. Within fifteen years, the *Short Course* sold forty-two million copies, was reprinted three hundred times, and was translated into sixty-seven languages. In the Russian edition, Stalin's name did not appear on the cover, and it was assumed that a committee had composed it, but Stalin clearly had scrutinized the work with care. After World War II, he claimed to be the author and the English edition carries his name on the cover.

The work abounds in vindictiveness toward his opponents, particularly his archenemy, Trotsky. It claims that at the Tenth Party Congress in 1921, which dealt in large part with the country's economic woes, 'The Trotskyites did not make a single definite proposal for the improvement of agriculture or industry, for the improvement of the circulation of commodities, or for the improvement of the condition of the working people. This did not even interest them.' On the other hand, it contains nothing but praise for Lenin, whose every decision was correct. There is no hint that Stalin might have had any differences with Lenin. And Stalin himself is lauded unstintingly: he is described as the 'Leader of Genius of the Proletarian Revolution', 'Inspirer and Organizer of the Victory of Socialism', and 'Supreme Genius of Humanity'. In a different publication, the poet Alexei Tolstoy, a distant relative of the novelist Leo Tolstoy, wrote the following in praise of Stalin:

> Thou, bright sun of the nations
> The unsinking sun of our times,
> And more than the sun, for the sun lacks wisdom.

To indoctrinate students with the principles of Bolshevism and inform them of Bolshevik successes, communist authorities made a special effort to establish new educational institutions. By 1928, over forty thousand party schools and study groups had been created to educate people in communist ideology, and to prepare them for possible membership of the Communist Party. At the same time, party cells were formed in universities, but in higher education the government had to exercise a degree of caution. Not enough trained scholars were available for the universities to be quickly turned into institutions serving the interests of the state. In 1921, a start was made to rectify this deficiency; the Red Professors' Institute was founded to produce university lecturers committed to communism. Within three years, ten 'communist universities' were created, and by 1928 the number had risen to nineteen; all told, eighty-four thousand students attended these institutions, which specialized in the social sciences, history, and philosophy. Within thirty years, over eight hundred institutions of higher education had been established; of these, sixty-nine were universities that offered full programs of study, that is, they trained a large number of students in the traditional fields of study. The contributions of graduates in the sciences have been especially impressive.

Soviet leaders often boasted that they had made enormous progress in modernizing their country and had made it possible for numerous citizens to lead interesting and productive lives. These achievements, many Soviet leaders claimed, entitled them to make an additional boast, that they had created a democracy superior to all others. But among those who opposed Stalin there was considerable doubt about this claim, as is suggested by the following joke that disaffected people used to tell each other: 'Under the dictatorship of the proletariat, two, three or even four parties may exist, but on condition that one is in power and all the rest in prison.'

What kind of social and political system did Stalin impose on Russia? Was it a revival of the tsarist autocracy? Was it a modern type of authoritarian regime, under which political power rests in the hands of one person, and a large proportion of the people are neither serf nor free? Or was it a new political order that some scholars have designated as totalitarian? Before an answer is offered, it might be best to examine the Constitution of 1936, which Stalin praised as the most democratic in the world, even though he acknowledged that in the Soviet Union only one party could be formed, for which he gave the following explanation: freedom for several parties 'exists only in a society in which there are antagonistic classes whose interests are mutually hostile and irreconcilable ... In the USSR there is ground for only one party.'

To grasp the essence of the political structure created by the new Constitution, it is useful to recall the analysis set forth by

Merle Fainsod in 1953 in his classic work *How Russia Is Ruled*, which was initially widely accepted as an accurate description of Stalinist rule. Fainsod argued that the Soviet regime rested on three pillars: the Communist Party, which controlled the indoctrination of the masses as well as the 'entire social order'; the secret police, which used repressive measures to prevent any form of opposition to the party; and the political and social elite, the *nomenklatura*, which, as already noted, held the major positions in the administration, the economy, the army, and the cultural institutions and, in addition, enjoyed far-reaching privileges denied to the vast majority of the population.

The Communist Party, known also as the 'vanguard of the proletariat', was assigned the task of directing every institution in the Soviet Union. In Stalin's words, the party was to issue the 'guiding directions' on policies, which were then to be implemented by the soviets, local organs of authority that the government could rely upon because it managed the elections of their members.Voters were presented with only one candidate and they faced the choice of publicly casting their votes for that person or of entering a booth watched carefully by local members of the party and replacing the candidate's name with one of their own choice. Not many people took the risk of voting in privacy.

Only citizens who had demonstrated their loyalty to the political system could expect to become a member of the Communist Party. The screening process began early in the lives of Soviet citizens. Children, known as *Little Octobrists*, began their political education in kindergarten and at the age of nine they joined the *Young Pioneers*, whose political education became more rigorous. Five years later, the youngsters were subjected to careful scrutiny and if they showed promise they were enrolled in the *Komsomol*, the organization entrusted with their political education until they reached the age of twenty-six.

The young people were expected to demonstrate that they could serve as model Soviet citizens. The twelve years in the

Komsomol were demanding, but there was no shortage of applicants because the prize of success was substantial. Those who were chosen for full membership of the Communist Party could count on successful careers. Not many people passed all the hurdles; in 1933, party membership reached 3.5 million out of a total population of about 170 million, but once persons had been selected for the promotion there was still no guarantee that they would spend their entire professional lives in secure and well-paying jobs. As already indicated, during the 1930s party membership fluctuated widely.

The central authorities in Moscow, and specifically Stalin and his close subordinates who were often members of the Politburo, relied heavily on local party members to publicize and enforce the directives emanating from the capital. The Communist Party's guiding principle was *democratic centralism*, but the primary emphasis was on centralism rather than democracy. Although all party institutions were elected and were obliged to issue periodic reports on their work, strict discipline was enforced: the decisions of the highest authorities in Moscow were in effect orders to the local officials. Criticism by members in the lower ranks of the party hierarchy of decisions reached by higher organs was strictly prohibited.

By itself, the Communist Party could not handle the implementation of Stalin's policies because most of its members held daytime jobs; they attended to political work in evenings and during weekends. To provide itself with full-time party workers, the government created a cadre known as *apparatchiki* or functionaries who devoted themselves solely to carrying out the orders from Moscow. Between 1925 and 1952, the number of full-time functionaries is estimated to have risen from 25,000 to 194,000. Their task was to inform local party members of the wishes of the government and, equally important, to recommend individuals who had proven their reliability and competence for promotion not only in the party hierarchy but also in the economic sphere, trade unions, agriculture, and so forth. The party functionaries received much higher salaries – in some cases fifty percent higher – than those in comparable positions in other branches of the government.

Fainsod was satisfied that his description of the structure of the Stalinist regime drew an accurate picture of the Soviet Union's political institutions, but he acknowledged that by itself it did not get to grips with the essential character of the political system, which he described as a totalitarian dictatorship. In making this point, he adopted a position that for about three decades was widely accepted by Western scholars of Stalinist rule.

Actually, two years before Fainsod's book appeared, Hannah Arendt, a philosopher, had published *The Origins of Totalitarianism*, in which she argued that both the Soviet Union and Nazi Germany were totalitarian states. Her book was widely acclaimed in academic circles and by people generally interested in the two major dictatorial regimes in the first half of the twentieth century.

Then, in 1972, the British scholar Leonard Schapiro delineated what he called the main contours of the political systems of the Soviet Union, Nazi Germany and Fascist Italy, all of which, he contended, were totalitarian. In each one, the Leader was an absolute ruler who had the final say not only on political, legal and military matters but also in the cultural sphere. Citizens who opposed the dictator or who appeared to do so were punished without regard for the rules of law. In each of the three countries, the Leader retained the fiction of democratic rule either by staging elections or organizing mass demonstrations of popular support. Finally, Schapiro pointed out that under totalitarianism there prevailed a 'fever of constant mobilization. Everyone is at all times being galvanized, dragooned, exhorted, shamed or compelled to act for some end or other.'

Not every Western scholar of Soviet history and Soviet politics agrees that totalitarianism is an appropriate description of the Stalinist system of rule. In fact, by the 1980s a substantial number of scholars, known as revisionists, considered the term misleading because it failed to take into account the complexity of the political order in the Soviet Union. A major failing of the totalitarian school, the revisionists argued, was its focus on politics and disregard for social history, whose approach yielded a more nuanced and hence a more accurate view of the Soviet Union. Several revisionists suspect that some of their colleagues in the totalitarian camp were motivated less by a search for truth than a desire to defame the Soviet Union. The controversy between the two camps became so intense that at one social gathering in the early 1980s two senior scholars almost came to blows – it took a great effort on the part of the professor who thought that the Soviet Union had been maligned to restrain himself.

Since the early 1990s several archives in the Russian Federation (formerly the Soviet Union) have been opened to Western scholars, some of whom have published articles and books that in their view contain evidence undermining the validity of the totalitarian model. These revisionists contend that the information they have found yields a more accurate description than was previously available of Stalinism, of the institutions of the Soviet Union, and, perhaps most important, of the attitude of a wide range of citizens in the USSR toward the communist system of rule.

Before summarizing in more detail the contents of some of these publications it is important to note that the concept of totalitarianism was not the invention of Western scholars of Stalinism. In 1925, Benito Mussolini, the Fascist dictator of Italy from 1922 to 1943, was the first political leader to use the term when he proudly claimed that he was turning Italy into a totalitarian state, which, as he put it, would be guided by the dogma of 'Everything for the state, nothing outside the state, nothing against the state.' Then, during the 1930s, the Western press and occasionally Western diplomats used the term to describe the political system of Nazi Germany.

Even though the concept of totalitarianism was not invented to besmirch the Soviet Union, the revisionists deserve a hearing. Their criticisms may be debatable, but they have raised important questions, and in the end it may well be that their archival research has yielded information that has deepened our understanding of Stalinism.

Professor Sheila Fitzpatrick was one of the first scholars to raise doubts about the validity of the totalitarian model. In a thoughtful article in *History and Theory*, she presented a detailed analysis of the disagreements between the traditionalists and the revisionists. The revisionists, she contended, charge that the traditionalists view Stalin's state as a 'completely top down entity' in which the masses were 'powerless [and] passive', totally at the mercy of the authorities in Moscow, whose 'main mechanism was terror, with propaganda used as a mobilizing device in second place'.

Some of the revisionists, who are predominantly social historians, have gone so far as to accuse the advocates of the totalitarian model having been 'corrupted by [their dependence] on government support', which, it is implied, was offered on the assumption that recipients would come up with scholarly works supporting their donors' views of the Soviet Union. In short, the traditionalists were said to produce scholarship that served the interests of their governments in the Cold War.

The revisionists, however, relying on information found in Russian archives, contended that the documents they studied supported their 'bottom-up' approach in analyzing Stalinism, that is, that the citizens of the Soviet Union were not as passive as the traditionalists assumed. The revisionists claimed to have found ample evidence in support of the following conclusions: the Soviet Union was not a completely monolithic state, and ideology was not the only factor guiding the country's leaders. Some also claimed to have found evidence that Stalin did not personally initiate the terror, and they firmly maintain that no precise figures on the number of victims during the Stalin era have been established. The implication is that Western scholars may well have exaggerated the suffering of the Soviet population.

Finally, the revisionists argued 'that somebody must be getting something out of this system, i.e. there must be some kind of social support for the regime'. Or, as Fitzpatrick put it in an article on revisionism in October 2008, 'With regard to popular support for Stalinism, it seemed to me unlikely that the regime survived on terror alone, but who supported the regime, who did not, and why, was what we did not know and wanted to find out.'

The theme that Stalin and Stalinism enjoyed substantial support in the Soviet Union is central to the work of the revisionists, and no one has developed this notion more elegantly than Professor Jochen Hellbeck, who in his research had access to a number of diaries stored in archives in the Russian Federation. In his book *Revolution on My Mind*, Hellbeck argued that the diaries showed that the government enjoyed the support of Soviet citizens, although no one knows what percentage of the population looked kindly upon the Stalinist regime. Hellbeck's point is that even some people who had suffered at the hands of the Soviet police were deeply committed to socialism and, as he put it, these men and women had fashioned their 'Stalinist souls' in conformity with the expectations of the Communist Party. Consequently, Hellbeck contends that the violence committed by the police in the 1930s and 1940s does not fully explain Stalin's success in radically changing the economic, social and political order.

Hellbeck, together with the historian Igal Halfin, first developed this thesis in an article in the *Jahrbücher für Geschichte Osteuropa* in 1996, in which they contended that the 'totalitarian interpretation' of the Stalinist regime 'reduced Soviet society to a victim of the regime's aspirations – a guinea pig at the disposal of all-powerful engineers'. Or, as they rephrased that point, many scholars of the Soviet Union had made the mistake of overlooking a 'key aspect of Bolshevism, namely, its desire to engage individuals with their soul. The goal of Bolshevik ideology ... was to make people understand the Communist program, in order to identify it and adopt it as their own.' In the authors' view, the communists succeeded in this endeavor to a greater extent than is generally recognized.

J. Arch Getty, Professor of History at the University of California, Los Angeles, is one of the most vigorous opponents of the 'totalitarian school'. In his book *Origins of the Great Purges: The Soviet Communist Party Reconsidered, 1933–1938*, he argued that the traditionalists had greatly exaggerated the purges and the importance in shaping Soviet policy of Stalin's 'diseased psyche', the term he dismissively applied to their concept of the leader's personality.

Getty suggested that instead of dwelling on Stalin's personal traits in explaining the history of the Soviet Union, scholars should pay more attention to party leaders at the local level, who favored purges to reduce their dependence on the communist leadership in Moscow. Getty also claimed that the punishments meted out to people found guilty of political misdemeanors had been exaggerated; most of them were simply expelled from the Communist Party.

Interestingly, Fitzpatrick, who probably wrote more than any other historian on the perceived flaws of the totalitarian school, recently published an engaging book, *On Stalin's Team: The Years of Living Dangerously in Soviet Politics*, that appears to mark something of a shift in her thinking about the nature of Stalin's rule. She does not focus on social history or, to put it differently, on a 'bottom-up' analysis of the communist system of government. Instead, she concentrates on how political decisions were reached at the highest level of authority in the Soviet Union. She argues that Stalin relied, to a much larger extent than has been realized, on a small group of close associates, all of whom occupied senior positions in the Communist Party. He regularly met with this group, discussed issues with them, and often took their advice into account.

This mode of rule seems to undermine the claims of the proponents of the totalitarian model, who maintain, as Fitzpatrick puts it, that the Soviet 'regime [was] headed by a charismatic leader, ruling through a mobilizing party aspiration and a secret police force, and aspiring to total control over society... [in short] Stalin's rule is often described as a personal dictatorship.' Professor Fitzpatrick notes that she has written extensively on this subject – as is indicated above in this book – and that she has been very critical of this interpretation of Stalinism. But she insists that for her present study of Stalin's form of government, the totalitarian 'model's relevance is quite limited, as it never focused on Stalin's relationship with his closest advisers or attached particular importance to it'.

Yet Professor Fitzpatrick is too good a historian to leave it at that. In several sections of this book she points out that although Stalin discussed issues with his team, he was clearly the person who wielded ultimate authority. On various pages she refers to him as the 'lynchpin of the whole thing', as the 'unchallengeable top dog', and, in addition, points out that the 'big policy initiatives were his'. She also indicates that he played the leading role in unleashing and directing the terror in the 1930s. For example, when Lazar Kaganovich, a long-standing member of the team, traveled to various localities in the Soviet Union to 'purge the local party committees' he checked in 'several times a day with Stalin in Moscow' to report on his progress in carrying out his mission. Moreover, Stalin 'was a suspicious man. He was suspicious even of his own team ... He kept tabs on them, encouraging informing, liked to keep them off balance and sometimes set traps for them ... Nobody on the team could feel safe.' 'As long as ... [Stalin] was alive' he 'still had the power to kill'.

Professor Richard Pipes, a leading proponent of the totalitarian model, published a distinctly favorable review of Fitzpatrick's book in the *New York Review of Books* of 5 December 2015, which he almost certainly would not have done for any of her previous works. For good reason, he found her book interesting and informative, and declared that the kind of 'revisionism' she espoused in this book was acceptable because it does not 'invalidate the totalitarian concept'.

Readers will have to decide whether the traditionalists or revisionists offer the most compelling description of Stalinism. More specifically, they will have to decide whether the existence of sizable groups of believers in the Bolshevik enterprise undermines the designation of the Soviet Union as a totalitarian state. In contemplating this question, they should keep in mind that no political system reflects perfectly its formal designation. No doubt, there were many Soviet citizens who, convinced of the soundness of Stalin's policies and ultimate goals, supported him. At the same time, some Soviet citizens may have considered it wiser to remain silent if they had reservations about the government's conduct of affairs, a possibility suggested in a previous chapter. Nor should patriotism be excluded as a possible explanation. Finally, by itself the existence of some public support for a political order should not be the critical factor in designating the character of that political system. There were no polls in nineteenth-century Russia, but there is considerable evidence to suggest that many peasants looked kindly upon their Tsar. But that does not mean that the political system of the Russian Empire was anything but a rigid and insensitive autocracy.

8
World War II, 1939–1945

The events leading to World War II and the Soviet Union's resistance to the invasion by Nazi Germany in 1941 brought out the best and the worst in Joseph Stalin as a political analyst and political operator. He misjudged Adolf Hitler from the moment he emerged as a major candidate for the leadership of Germany in 1932, primarily because the Soviet leader lacked a sound grasp of German politics. His central miscalculation was his belief that German fascism was the highest form of imperialism and capitalism and that Hitler would not remain in power very long; the masses, Stalin insisted, would rise up against him and would bring the communists to power. It was this conviction that guided the Soviet leader late in 1932, when the German Social Democrats, who more thoroughly understood the political situation in their country, were so desperate for communist support in the upcoming election that they raised the question of collaboration between their party and the communists with officials at the Soviet Embassy in Berlin. After several meetings, they were told by the Soviet Embassy attaché, Boris Vinogradov, that 'Moscow is convinced that the road to Soviet Germany leads through Hitler.'

This message from Moscow amounted to a repetition of orders the Kremlin had sent to the German Communist Party in the summer of 1931; at that time, officials in Moscow directed the German communists to support a plebiscite that the Nazis and other right-wingers were proposing for the purpose of undermining the Social Democratic government in Prussia. This move was part and parcel of Stalin's policy, announced in 1930, of seeking to undermine the German Social Democrats, whom the communists chose to call 'social-fascists'. It would be misleading to contend that Stalin bore responsibility for Nazism's triumph, but there is little doubt that he did not do all he could to hinder Hitler's rise to power.

After 1933, Stalin's attitude toward Hitler and Nazi Germany was in some important respects ambiguous and even contradictory. On several occasions, he indicated that he did not regard Hitler as a menace to Europe and that he did not consider even some of his most reprehensible actions as vile. Like so many other political leaders of the 1920s and 1930s, Stalin failed to take seriously Hitler's pronouncements in his most significant publication, *Mein Kampf*, where, among other things, he set forth his views of Marxism and the Soviet Union. Apparently, Stalin did not understand that politicians of the right could be as committed to ideology as politicians of the left. A few quotations from Hitler's book, published in two volumes in 1925 and 1927, will help the reader understand the extent to which many of Stalin's views and actions with regard to Nazism were misguided:

> Let no one argue that in concluding an alliance with Russia we need not immediately think of war, or, if we did, that we could thoroughly prepare for it. *An alliance whose aim does not embrace a plan for war is senseless and worthless ... The present rulers of Russia have no idea of honorably entering into an alliance, let alone observing one.*
>
> ...
>
> Never forget that the rulers of present-day Russia are common blood-stained criminals; that they are the scum of humanity, which, favored by circumstances, overran a great state in a tragic hour, slaughtered and wiped out thousands

of her leading intelligentsia in wild blood lust, and now for almost ten years have been carrying on the most cruel and tyrannical regime of all time ... Do not forget that the international Jew who completely dominates Russia today regards Germany, not as an ally, but as a state destined to the same fate. And you do not make pacts with anyone whose sole interest is the destruction of his partner ... In Russian Bolshevism we must see the attempt undertaken by the Jews in the twentieth century to achieve world domination ... *The fight against Jewish world Bolshevization requires a clear attitude toward Soviet Russia. You cannot drive out the devil with Beelzebub.*

Despite Hitler's disdain for the Soviet Union, Stalin admired the way Hitler disposed of his opponents. Most notably, Stalin approved of Hitler's order that Ernst Röhm be murdered. Röhm headed the Brownshirts, a special Nazi organization he was eager to integrate into the army. The army and its leadership would have been markedly weakened if Röhm had succeeded, and he would have been in a position to challenge Hitler for the leadership of the country. Publicly, Röhm expressed loyalty to Hitler, but privately he voiced many criticisms of the Führer.

Röhm had been a close comrade of Hitler ever since the early 1920s, but he did not hide his sense of superiority to the Führer, who had served as a mere corporal in the army during World War I, whereas Röhm had been a captain. Hitler decided to eliminate Röhm as a threat, and while he was at it he decided to eliminate many other people he considered potential threats to his authority. On 30 June 1934, in what was later known as the Night of the Long Knives, his henchmen, under his orders, murdered at least seventy-seven senior officials in the National Socialist Party and several political leaders such as General Kurt von Schleicher, a right-winger who had served briefly as Chancellor in 1932. Röhm was among the victims.

Stalin avidly read all the reports on the massacre sent to Moscow by Soviet secret agents. At a meeting of the Politburo shortly after he received news of Hitler's elimination of potential rivals, he said:'Have you heard what happened in Germany? Some fellow that Hitler. Knows how to treat his political opponents.'

It may be that Hitler's firm handling of suspected opponents caused Stalin to change his mind about the likelihood of a proletarian revolution in Germany in the foreseeable future. It is also possible that the Soviet leader was alarmed by the signing of a non-aggression treaty by Germany and Poland in 1934. Poland, after all, had a long history of unfriendly relations with its powerful neighbor in the east. Whatever the reason, in 1934 Stalin began to view Germany as a military threat and in September of that year the Soviet Union, eager to secure support from other countries in international crises, joined the League of Nations. In addition, Stalin now supported the so-called Popular Front Policy, which favored a coalition in the West of left-wing parties with non-socialist liberal parties against fascism. In the spring of 1935, the communist leadership in the Soviet Union publicly expressed concern about Germany's program of rearmament. An article in *Pravda* for the first time pointed out that in *Mein Kampf*, Hitler had adopted an aggressive tone toward the Soviet Union. The article also warned that in a few months the German army would consist of 849,000 trained men, forty percent more than the French army and 'nearly as many as the 949,000 under arms in the Soviet Union'. At this time, Stalin was eager to join forces with Western powers with a view to building a 'collective security' system against any aggressor.

But at roughly the same time, Stalin indicated interest in establishing good relations with Nazi Germany. A series of friendly meetings between David Kandelaki, head of a Soviet mission to Berlin, and Herbert L. W. Göring, a cousin of the second most powerful Nazi, Hermann Göring, resulted in the conclusion of an economic agreement beneficial to both countries. Stalin was pleased and now felt confident that the Soviet Union's relations with Germany would henceforth be friendly. 'Well, now,' he said to a meeting of the Politburo, 'how can Hitler make war on us if he has granted us loans? It's impossible.'

The two dictators, Hitler and Stalin, had hidden motives in accepting the agreement. Hitler had no intention of abiding by it for long, but the agreement was useful in giving Germany time to prepare for war. In fact, in mid-August 1936, Hitler drafted a secret memorandum in which he declared that war with the Soviet Union was inevitable. He noted that Germany's rapid population increase and its need for raw materials left the country no alternative to expansion in the East. He put Hermann Göring in charge of a Four Year Plan to prepare Germany for war. Stalin did not know that such a plan existed and saw no reason not to continue to woo Germany. He thought it likely that Germany would wage war against Western powers, a struggle that would weaken the Western capitalist countries, giving the Soviet Union time to strengthen itself economically and militarily. The eventual result would be the weakening of capitalism and the strengthening of socialism. This calculation by Stalin was a fundamental consideration for him in shaping the foreign policy of the Soviet Union in the years from 1936 to 1941.

That Hitler planned an aggressive foreign policy became clear soon after he solidified his power as dictator of Germany. In 1933, he abandoned the League of Nations; two years later he violated the military clauses of the Versailles Treaty by substantially enlarging Germany's armed forces; and in 1936, he ordered his troops to reoccupy the Rhineland (also in violation of the Versailles Treaty). The aggressive moves continued in the spring of 1938 when German forces entered Austria and incorporated it into Germany. Later that year, Western diplomats at Munich agreed to Hitler's annexation of the Sudetenland, which was part of Czechoslovakia; and early in 1939, Germany seized the rest of Czechoslovakia. Only after Germany attacked Poland, on

1 September 1939, did France and Great Britain decide to put a
halt to Hitler's aggression by declaring war on 3 September.

Stalin stood on the sidelines during the parade of Hitler's
aggressive moves in the late 1930s because he became more
convinced than ever that it was to his country's advantage for
the major European powers to exhaust themselves in a military
conflict. Even the invasion by Germany of Czechoslovakia did
not evoke any strong measures by the Soviet Union. More
surprising to Western governments and even to radicals in the
West who were sympathetic to communism, Stalin concluded an
elaborate pact with Nazi Germany. The first steps were taken in
1938 and these led to an agreement a year later. In April 1939,
Alexei F. Merekalov, the Soviet ambassador in Berlin, assured
Ernst von Weizsäcker, the State Secretary of the German Foreign
Ministry, that 'ideological differences need not be a stumbling
block to Russian–German relations,' which, he said, could be put
on a sound footing. Stalin eased the way to improving relations
between the two countries on 3 May 1939, when he discharged
Maxim Litvinov as Foreign Commissar and replaced him with
Vyacheslav Molotov. Litvinov was a Jew and it would have been
distasteful to Hitler and his government to deal with him.

In the meantime, Britain and France, fearful of facing
Germany alone, took some half-hearted steps to win Stalin over.
The Russian negotiators made it clear that their country would
enter into a defensive agreement with Britain and France only
if the Soviet Union were granted the right to station troops in
the buffer states on its border, that is, Poland, Romania, Finland,
Estonia, and Lithuania. All those countries refused. Nevertheless, on 11 August 1939, after a leisurely trip, an Anglo-French
delegation arrived in Moscow to negotiate a pact on military
collaboration between their countries and Stalin. But the negotiations collapsed on 22 August, when the Soviet authorities
announced that they had reached an agreement with Germany
on a non-aggression pact. Some scholars have argued that the

Western powers could have struck a deal with the Soviet Union had they acted with greater speed and determination. Others, however, have expressed strong doubts about Stalin's willingness to collaborate with the West in calling a halt to Hitler's advances. 'What ... [Stalin] sought', according to Tucker, was to encourage a protracted war 'pitting ... the Western democracies against Germany, a war in which the USSR would be uninvolved, or only insignificantly involved, while recovering from the havoc caused by his Terror and positioning itself to intervene at a time of his choosing in order to carry on its revolution into Eastern Europe and the Balkans'.

The non-aggression agreement signed by the Soviet Union and Germany, and Stalin's subsequent determination to abide by all its provisions regardless of numerous violations by the Nazis, certainly support Tucker's contention. So does Stalin's statement issued after Great Britain together with France declared war on Germany on 3 September 1939, in which he insisted, as Tucker put it, that the 'war was ... a conflict between rival imperialisms in which the [Communist] parties' duty was to deny their governments [that were involved in the war] support and work for a negotiated peace'. What Stalin did not reveal was that his agreement with the Nazi regime obligated the Soviet Union to send much-needed supplies to Germany, which meant that a communist country was aiding the war effort of a fascist state.

When some of the details of the agreement became public – quite a few were not revealed – many people of all political persuasions were stunned. The pact, which was to last ten years, gave Hitler a free hand to attack Poland, and several secret provisions stipulated that after Poland's defeat, Eastern Europe would be divided between Germany and the Soviet Union. Finland, Estonia, and Latvia were placed in the Soviet sphere of influence and the Soviet Union was also given carte blanche to annex Bessarabia. Other sections of the pact provided for extensive trade between the two countries, which would be especially beneficial to

Germany's war effort. Hitler was overjoyed when he received news by telephone from Joachim von Ribbentrop, his lead negotiator in Moscow, that a final agreement had been reached. And so was Stalin; at a reception marking the successful conclusion of the negotiations, Stalin offered the following toast: 'I know how much the German people love their Führer. I would therefore like to drink to his health.' Stalin firmly believed that he had outsmarted Hitler, and his confidence in the longevity of the agreement was bolstered a few months later, when the Germans told Molotov that after Britain's defeat, Russia would be assigned some of the lands controlled by the British Empire. To those who criticized the agreement, Stalin's supporters had a ready answer: they blamed the Poles for the Soviet Union's failure to reach an agreement with the West. They claimed that under the circumstances they had no choice but to sign the pact with Germany.

Actually, Stalin had persuaded himself that the agreement served the mutual interests of Germany and the Soviet Union. Late in September 1939, a few weeks after the pact was signed, he told Ribbentrop that 'Soviet foreign policy was always based on the belief in the possibility of cooperation between Germany and the Soviet Union ... Historically, the Soviet Government never excluded the possibility of good relations with Germany. Hence it is with a clear conscience that the Soviet Government begins the revival of collaboration with Germany. This collaboration represents a power that the other combinations must give into.'

Stalin was so determined to please the Germans that during the two years from 1939 to mid-1941 he made sure that the promised supplies of grain, ore, and other materials were sent to Germany even though early in 1941 the Germans stopped shipping machine tools and other items they had promised the Russians.

In the meantime, on 1 September 1939, Hitler had launched the invasion of Poland and after easily defeating the ill-equipped Polish forces, within three weeks the German army occupied close to one half of the country, the western part up to the Narew, Vistula, and San rivers. The eastern sector was occupied by the Soviet army, which began its march into Poland on 17 September, as stipulated in secret sections of the Russo-German Pact.

The Russians proceeded to impose a Soviet-style political regime on the Poles, including waging a vigorous campaign against suspected opponents of communism. The most notorious incident was the massacre in April 1940 in Katyn Forest, near Smolensk, of about fifteen thousand Polish officers, as well as policemen, intellectuals, professors, landowners, and priests, who had been taken prisoner during the war and after the conclusion of hostilities. The purpose of the killings was to forestall the Poles from organizing resistance to the invaders. When evidence of the massacre came to light in 1943, the Russians claimed that German soldiers had been the perpetrators. Fifty years later, in 1990, officials in Moscow acknowledged that Stalin had given the order for the executions and that Beria had been involved in planning them.

For about eight months, the western front, where French and British troops faced the German army, remained fairly quiescent; the only major military action took place in the east between the Soviet Union and Finland. Lithuania, Latvia, and Estonia had yielded to Stalin's demands that Soviet garrisons be stationed in their countries, but the Finns, who agreed to give up some land in return for concessions by the Russians elsewhere, refused to accede to one specific demand, that the Soviet Union be granted a base near Hanko, a town in western Finland. On 30 November 1939, after two months of futile negotiations, Stalin ordered his troops to invade Finland. It is not clear whether Stalin had planned military action against Finland all along, but once the fighting began it became apparent that he intended to occupy the entire country. He had fully expected the war to be short, just like Hitler's in Poland. But the Finnish army put up fierce resistance, while the Soviet forces turned out to be incompetent, for reasons discussed below, and could not score the decisive victories they had anticipated. Stalin decided to negotiate an end to the war in March 1940, and the only concessions granted by the Finns were those they had offered before hostilities began.

The failure to deliver a knockout blow to the Finns made Stalin realize that the Soviet army needed extensive improvement. Commanders took steps to intensify the training of soldiers, and ministers in charge of industry focused on the production of more effective tanks and weapons, but fifteen months later, when Hitler invaded Russia, these measures turned out to have been woefully inadequate.

It did not take the Soviet leaders long to realize that the German military machine was even more efficient than had been assumed after their lightning victory in Poland. In May 1940, the so-called phony war in the West, during which both sides avoided a major confrontation, came to an end with the Nazi invasion of Holland, Belgium, and France, and within a matter of weeks the Germans crushed the armies of all three. According to Khrushchev, on hearing the news of France's defeat and Britain's hasty retreat from the country to avoid having its army taken prisoner by the Germans, 'Stalin's nerves cracked ... He cursed the governments of England and France. "Couldn't they put up any resistance at all?" he asked despairingly.' His expectation that a war between Germany and the Western powers would weaken all the major capitalist states had turned out to be mistaken. Hitler had proven the military superiority of Germany, and he had established himself as the master of Europe. Stalin feared that if the Germans attacked the Soviet Union, they would be able 'to beat our brains in'.

But that was not Hitler's aim at that time. In a state of ecstasy over his easy victory against France, he thought it best to complete the conquest of Western Europe. He turned his attention to Great Britain and tried to conclude a peace treaty that would consist of two major provisions: Britain would be permitted to hold on to its empire and Hitler would become the leader of all of Europe. Prime Minister Winston Churchill would not hear of it. A few months later, on 13 August 1940, the Germans unleashed a series of air attacks known as Operation Eagle, which was designed to bring the country to its knees by destroying the British air force and bombing civilian targets in major cities to demoralize the populace, who would then press the government to give in. But the British air force and the British people refused to buckle. After nine months it was clear that attacks from the air alone would not succeed, and apparently the Germans lacked sufficient sea power to invade Britain. Hitler then looked to the East.

Over a period of about six months, indications that Germany was preparing an assault on the Soviet Union were so numerous and vivid that Stalin's refusal to take any of them seriously is baffling. Early in 1941, Soviet intelligence officials warned Stalin that the Germans were making elaborate preparations for an attack. The historian Robert Gellately recently noted that during a six-month period in the first half of that year those officials sent the Kremlin 'fifty-six intelligence reports … each growing more specific'. They even supplied Stalin with four dates that had been chosen for the beginning of hostilities: 6 April, 20 April, 18 May, or 22 June, all in 1941. Stalin responded to these warnings by asking Hitler about the masses of German troops assembling in Poland, and the Führer replied that the soldiers were stationed in the East to protect them from Western bombing attacks and to keep them in shape for attacks against Britain. Stalin was satisfied with the response.

It was also known that the *Luftwaffe*, the German air force, had conducted no fewer than 180 'unauthorized flights' over Soviet territory. The reaction of the authorities in Moscow to this information was strange. The Soviet Press Agency published an article on 14 June 1941, eight days before the German invasion, denying the reports as 'rumors spread by forces hostile to the Soviet Union and Germany'. At the same time, British and American officials informed the Kremlin that they had solid information that Hitler was planning to invade, but Stalin paid no heed. Finally, at the last minute before the attack, a German deserter told a Soviet officer that German troops would launch an attack at dawn on 22 June. The information reached Marshal Semyon Timoshenko and he, together with the Chief of Staff, General Gyorgy Zhukov, passed the information on to Stalin. On their own authority, the two officers ordered Soviet units at the border to be on the alert. But even then Stalin dismissed the news as 'a provocation', and only after the generals pressed the General Secretary did he author-ize the issuance of an alert to the troops. Stalin simply did not believe that Hitler would break his pact with him. At 3:15 A.M. on 22 June, the German army crossed the frontier and only when Stalin heard of the invasion was he finally convinced that the Nazi leader had violated the agreements with the Soviet Union.

The news of the German invasion was so unexpected in the Kremlin that Soviet freight trains carrying supplies of grain and fuel were on their way to Nazi-occupied lands at the moment German troops launched their assault on territories controlled by the communists.

How can one explain Stalin's refusal to heed the growing evidence that the Germans were on the verge of invading the Soviet Union? He had made up his mind that Hitler would not attack the Soviet Union, at least not in the foreseeable future, and he could not conceive of the possibility that he might be wrong. It did not occur to him that Hitler would betray him because that would have undermined Stalin's ideological understanding of international affairs, that is, that the capitalist countries would exhaust themselves in military conflicts and thus pave the way for the expansion of communism into Central and Western Europe. Stalin was definitely both intelligent and perspicacious, and very often he had demonstrated his gifts by outwitting his political rivals. But he was so self-righteous that at times he made deci-sions that were not wise.

If readers keep in mind this personal trait of Stalin, they will have no trouble understanding Stalin's conduct when it emerged beyond any doubt that he had been wrong and that the Soviet Union had been attacked without any provocation on its part. This man of steel – as his adopted name portrayed him – who had spent years in exile or jail, who had defeated leading party members in the struggle for leadership of the Soviet Union, who had consigned many thousands of people to death, and who had ordered the purge from the party of hundreds of thousands of innocent men and women and sent them to labor camps, collapsed from a nervous breakdown when he received incontrovertible evidence that German troops had attacked the country. A few days after the invasion, Stalin left the Defense Commissariat with Molotov, Gyorgy Malenkov, Voroshilov, Andrei Zhdanov, and Beria (all leading members of the government), and suddenly 'he burst out loudly: "Lenin left us a great heritage and we, his heirs, have fucked it all up!" Molotov looked at him amazed, but, like the others, said nothing.' Stalin was so paralyzed that in effect no one was in command and for five days, 25–29 June, the newspapers did not even print his name, an unprecedented omission in a country where the leader was mentioned constantly to remind the people that he, and he alone, made the final decisions on all issues of national importance. A country accustomed to taking orders from Tsars, and then from Lenin and Stalin, could not function effectively without being told what stand to adopt on major issues. And now, most important of all, they were not being advised on how to respond to the German invasion. 'In [Stalin's] absence', Adam Ulam noted, 'Russia ceased to be ruled.'

This abnormal state of affairs ended on 30 June, when Stalin returned to work. That day the 'State Defense Committee' was formed, consisting of Stalin as chairman and four other members (Molotov, Voroshilov, Beria, and Malenkov). Three days later, on 3 July, Stalin addressed the nation on the radio, the first time since the start of hostilities that he was able to muster the energy to rally the people to the defense of the country. It was not a stirring presentation and at one point, when he picked up a glass of water, his hand trembled. He defended his decision to sign a pact with the Nazis on the ground that no 'peace-loving country' could reject the offer of a treaty of non-aggression even if the offer came from leaders as 'perfidious and monstrous ... as Hitler and Ribbentrop'. The two years of peace, he insisted, had given the Soviet Union 'the opportunity to prepare ... [our] forces to repulse fascist Germany ... This is a definite advantage to us and a disadvantage to Germany.' He then thanked British Prime Minister Winston Churchill and the leaders of the United States, who only weeks earlier had been reviled in the Soviet press as malicious defenders of capitalism, for their offer of help.

But the most important part of the speech consisted of an appeal to the Soviet people to struggle relentlessly against the enemy. He singled out the residents of areas about to be surrendered to the Nazis and those of areas already occupied: he urged the former to engage in a scorched-earth policy and the latter to wage partisan warfare against the enemy. He called on the Red Army, the navy, and the nation as a whole to join in the effort to 'defeat the enemy'. He ended with the rallying cry 'Forward to our Victory!' All in all, it was not an inspiring speech, but many citizens were relieved that their leader had returned to his duties, and so were most senior officials, who regarded Stalin as the only person capable of running the country at this perilous moment.

The German army had launched a well-planned and relentless attack, which they named 'Barbarossa', against an opponent whose troops were poorly equipped and trained. Within the first nine hours of warfare, the Germans destroyed twelve hundred Soviet airplanes, two thirds of them while they were still on the ground. The Soviet generals ordered their troops to counterattack, but the men had not been prepared for offensive warfare. They were so inept that the Germans managed, without much effort, to surround many of the Soviet soldiers they encountered and to kill or capture them. After two days of fighting, Hitler's forces had advanced one hundred miles into Soviet territory. Three weeks later, the Germans were close to capturing Smolensk, about 220 miles from Moscow. Four weeks after that, another army was close to capturing Leningrad, the Soviet Union's second largest city, which until March 1918 had been the capital. And by the end of August, the Germans had entered Kiev, the capital of the Ukraine. Hitler's army reached the outskirts of Moscow early in the winter of 1941.

One reason for the rapid advance of the Germans was that Stalin, despite having unquestioned intelligence, the ability to master details, and the energy to work endless hours without much rest, did not trust his experienced officers, who knew more than he about military strategy and tactics. Moreover, he was inordinately stubborn, and once he had set his mind on a policy, his advisers were hard put to persuade him to change course. One of his biggest mistakes in the early stages of the war was to insist that every square foot of land must be defended; often, it is better to retreat than to fight, as the Russians had learned at the time of Napoleon's invasion about 125 years earlier. Marshal Zhukov, one of the country's ablest officers, was increasingly frustrated by Stalin's refusal to approve of 'timely withdrawals'. Zhukov quickly realized that, in addition to being ill-prepared for war, the Soviet troops were also not well deployed. He therefore contended that many of them should be moved to other regions, even if that meant abandoning some territory. But the marshal repeatedly had to bow to Stalin's orders.

Another mistake Stalin made in the early period of the war was to appoint incompetent officers to important positions at the front, though it was not entirely his fault. The government had failed to provide adequate training to officers; indeed, none of the regimental commanders had spent time at the Frunze Academy, the main institution for officer training. And as a result of the purges of the military in the 1930s, there was a general shortage of trained officers. Not surprisingly, among those who had survived the purges, quite a few were too timid to take the kind of initiatives necessary in time of battle. All these weaknesses of the Soviet military had been a major factor in the poor performance of troops in the war against Finland. Stalin's government had done little to correct the military deficiencies.

But Stalin's biggest mistakes undoubtedly were his failure to prepare the people for the sacrifices they would have to make in the event of war and his insufficient attention to increasing the production of weapons and other items such as tanks needed to wage a modern war. It has also been suggested that Stalin refused to order the mobilization of Soviet troops early in June because he remembered that in 1914 Tsar Nicholas's decision to mobilize Russian troops had been a major reason for Germany's moves toward a war footing. As already suggested, Stalin was desperate to avoid any action that could be interpreted by Hitler as a provocation.

The successes of the German army were not simply the result of superior training, better equipment, and more effective leadership. To the surprise of German officers, in parts of the Soviet Union, especially in the Ukraine, numerous citizens met the invaders with open arms. In his memoirs, General Heinz Guderian, one of Germany's most capable tank commanders, wrote of his surprise at the reception his troops received from the local population when his unit entered the area of Roslavl, a town in the Smolensk region about 220 miles southwest of Moscow: 'A significant indication of the attitude of the civilian population is provided by the fact that women came out of their villages on to the very battlefield bringing wooden platters of bread and butter and eggs and, in my case at least, refused to let me move on before I had eaten.' Actually, the reaction of ordinary citizens to the Germans is not all that surprising. Many of them, in particular the Ukrainians, had suffered terribly during the early 1930s, when famine added to the woes of collectivization. They now hoped that the Germans would restore the agricultural system of the pre-1928 era.

The average peasant in the Ukraine knew little about the political and social program of the Nazis, who would almost certainly have scored more lasting victories had they not been committed to racist views. Hitler, who in some respects turned out to be a more unyielding ideologue than Stalin, insisted on treating the Ukrainians as *Untermenschen* (subhumans). Hitler is quoted as having said of the region occupied by German troops: 'Naturally this giant area would have to be pacified. The best solution would have to be to shoot anyone who looks askance.' Within months of the beginning of the war, many people under Nazi rule had changed from sympathizers of the invaders to their enemies. Numerous bands were formed that specialized in attacks on German troops, who found it increasingly difficult to fight two wars at the same time, the Soviet soldiers in front of them and the partisans in the rear. General Guderian blamed his own countrymen for the change of heart by ordinary Russians. 'Unfortunately,' he recalled, '[the] friendly attitude toward the Germans lasted only so long as the more benevolent military administration was in control. The so-called "Reich commissars" soon managed to alienate all sympathy from the Germans and thus to prepare the ground for all the horrors of partisan warfare.' It may be an exaggeration to suggest that friendly treatment of local citizens in the occupied territories would have enabled the Nazis to defeat the Russians, but it would probably have made the war far more challenging for the Soviet Union.

In addition to being embarrassed by Soviet citizens' welcome of the German invaders, Soviet leaders were further distressed when General Andrei Vlasov, a highly regarded commander, defected to the Germans after having been captured on 12 July 1942. His reason for this act of treason is not clear; it seems that he had concluded that Stalin's military and political policies were ruining the country. Once he had changed sides, he proposed to German officials that he be permitted to form an army of captured Soviet soldiers and lead them in battle against the communist army. But Hitler balked because he did not trust any Russians. He refused to give Vlasov more than nominal support. It has been suggested that Hitler feared that if Vlasov played a key role in defeating the Soviet army, he would emerge as a political leader in the Soviet Union and then spoil Hitler's plan to seize control of large parts of the country. As it turned out, Vlasov's army did little fighting and, immediately after the war, United States officials refused to give Vlasov asylum and turned him over to Soviet authorities. The general was tried, found guilty, and immediately executed.

Unlike Hitler, Stalin showed considerable flexibility on ideological issues once he had recovered from his psychological collapse. In his effort to rouse Soviet citizens to devote their energies to the war effort and to make the ultimate sacrifice if necessary, he changed course on some major issues as well as in his behavior, which had always been rather gruff. In his public speeches he now addressed his countrymen as 'brothers and sisters' or 'my friends', in addition to greeting them with the more formal 'comrades' and 'citizens'. At public gatherings such as the celebration of the Revolution of 1917, he spoke less about Lenin and the triumphs of Bolshevism and much more about the achievements of such national heroes as Alexander Nevsky, a ruler in the thirteenth century, and Mikhail Kutuzov, the field marshal who defeated Napoleon in 1812. The press no longer emphasized achieving socialism, and focused instead on the glories of Russia; to be more precise, it appealed to nationalist sentiment, which had been derided in the early years after the Revolution of 1917. In this vein, Stalin went out of his way to demonstrate that he was truly a patriot, a man of steel, and the embodiment of 'courage and iron will'. In the press, a new national slogan appeared: 'For the Motherland! For Stalin!'

In short, after Stalin recovered from his nervous breakdown, he turned out to be highly effective in running the war effort, which became his overriding concern. He headed the Supreme Command (the *Stavka*) and chose competent men to serve as senior officers of the army, going so far as to search for gifted officers in various labor camps, to which they had been sent as punishment only a few years earlier, in most cases for no reason other than that they were suspected of not being sufficiently loyal to Stalin. Experienced officers were desperately needed partly because Stalin did not hesitate to dismiss commanders who had proven to be poor leaders in battles with the Germans.

In addition, although Stalin was an avowed atheist who had been determined to root out religion and had supported all the steps taken in the 1920s to emasculate religious institutions, he now took various steps to overcome the rift between the state and the Orthodox Church. He ordered government officials to stop issuing hostile propaganda against the Church, and he took the initiative in arranging a personal meeting with several leaders of the Church. 'No effort would be spared during the war,' according to Adam Ulam, 'to persuade the people that the regime had had a change of heart: the bad old days of the thirties would not return, victory would bring a new order, if not of freedom in the Western sense of the word, then of social peace.' In May 1943, Stalin moved to calm fears in the international community about the Soviet Union's future plans to agitate for revolution in the West and elsewhere by dissolving the Comintern, the organization devoted to promoting Bolshevik ideals outside the Soviet Union.

Stalin's tactics worked. The West, pleased to have another ally in the war against Hitler, sent huge quantities of military equipment and other needed items to the Soviet Union. And increasingly the Soviet people became aware of the barbarism of the Nazi invaders and demonstrated a degree of bravery and determination to defend their homeland that was justly lauded in all the countries aligned against Germany. Details of their suffering and passionate devotion to their country will be described below, but they need to be mentioned here to help the reader understand how it was possible for the Soviet Union to withstand the Nazi onslaught and ultimately repel the invaders.

For several months in 1941, the German juggernaut could not be stopped. Foreign troops occupied areas that were home to sixty million people – about thirty percent of the country's entire population – and that were vitally important economically. The Nazis seized control of the Ukraine, Belorussia, and the Baltic region and had even penetrated into sections of what was traditionally known as Russia. By mid-October, German troops had reached the outskirts of Moscow, but heavy rains slowed down the German tanks, giving the Soviet officials a chance to work on the defense of the city. By this time the losses on both sides had already been enormous: the Russians had suffered three million casualties and the Germans 750,000. But in a sense, the Germans found themselves in worse condition than their opponents. Hitler had predicted that the Soviet Union would be defeated by Christmas and would then be begging for mercy. It was one of his most costly miscalculations, especially since the Germans were unprepared to fight in the bitter cold of the Russian winter. The lack of appropriate equipment and clothing would also plague the Germans in a later, in some respects even more critical, battle.

Instead of begging for mercy, Soviet citizens hurriedly made extensive preparations to defend their capital. The most important moves were to bring a large contingent of troops from the Far East to the vicinity of Moscow, and to place it under the command of Marshal Zhukov, generally regarded as the Soviet Union's most capable commander. Still, the fear of being overrun by the Germans was so strong that the government and party agencies, and defense factories as well, were evacuated to Kuibyshev (formerly Samara on the Volga). It was rumored that for three days (16–19 October) Stalin himself had abandoned the city, but then he returned and immediately took charge of Moscow's defense. To be certain that the military would have a free hand in organizing the operation, he imposed martial law on the capital.

On 6 December 1941, Zhukov led a counteroffensive that was so carefully and intelligently planned and so well executed that within six weeks the Germans were forced to retreat 140 miles, placing them two hundred miles from the city. Zhukov's success did not drive the Germans out of the country, but it was a major defeat for the invaders, the first one of consequence since the beginning of the conflict six months earlier. Hitler was so distressed that he sacked Walther von Brauchitsch, the Commander in Chief, and appointed himself to that position, a major blunder because he was not a wise military strategist. He made the same mistake that Stalin had made early in the conflict: he refused to order tactical retreats when the opposing army held the advantage in a specific region. He repeated this mistake on other occasions, the most memorable being the Battle of Stalingrad, which took place about a year later. Whenever Hitler ordered his troops to stay put in the face of a superior military force, the Germans incurred huge and unnecessary losses. At the same time, the victory near Moscow greatly enhanced Stalin's reputation as a wartime leader and strengthened the determination of Soviet citizens to defend their country.

That determination was especially strong in Leningrad, the country's second most populous, and in some respects most honored, city, in large part because of its name. When German troops reached its outskirts early in September 1941, the resistance of both the military and the civilian population proved so heroic that however much they tried, the Germans could not crush the defenders. The invaders then blockaded the city with the aim of forcing the army and local residents to surrender. Food and medicines were in short supply, but the population did not cave in even though, according to the best estimates, about a million people out of a total of three million died during the siege, which lasted an astonishing 872 days, until 24 January 1944. By that time, the German army had lost several major battles in other parts of the country, and its troops had no choice but to retreat from the Leningrad area.

Germany's most devastating defeat, which marked a turning point in the war, occurred in Stalingrad, a city of about five hundred thousand inhabitants on the right bank of the Volga river in the southeastern region of European Russia. Its capture would have given Germany control of the Volga waterway and would thus have enabled Hitler to cut Russia off from its oil supply. But Hitler apparently had an additional reason for pressing the offensive, which began on 23 August 1942. He had persuaded himself that Stalingrad's fall would deliver a devastating psychological blow to Soviet citizens and perhaps even to the egocentric Stalin; after all, the city had been named for him and during the Civil War in 1918, when it was named Tsaritsyn, he had suffered one of his greatest political defeats at the hands of his archenemy, Trotsky.

Be that as it may, Stalin had ample reason to call for a robust defense of Stalingrad. In his order to the troops, he declared that under no circumstance should Stalingrad be surrendered: 'Not a single step backward … you have to fight to your last drop of blood to defend every position, every foot of Soviet soil.' The soldiers did just that, and Hitler once again committed the fatal error of refusing to withdraw when it was clear that Soviet fighters could not be dislodged from their positions. Several generals urged him to pull back to more defensible lines, but he ignored them. The 48th Panzer Corps, commanded by General Ferdinand Heim, was sent to relieve the pressure on the invaders, but his troops failed to dislodge the Russian troops closing in on the German army. Infuriated, the Führer fired Heim and ordered his subordinates to sentence him to death. Heim was saved by the intervention of a colleague.

Hitler then ordered General Friedrich Paulus, commander of the Sixth Army in the Stalingrad region, to persist in attacking the city; in no event was he to retreat or give up. To encourage the general, Hitler promoted him to Field Marshal. For over four months the battle raged, the fiercest of the entire war, and on 31 January 1943, Paulus, surrounded by Soviet troops and short of food, ammunition, and clothing, had no choice but to surrender. About 100,000 German troops had lost their lives and about 113,000 were taken prisoner, including Field Marshal Paulus. It was Germany's greatest defeat to date in World War II and it proved to be a turning point not only in the fighting in the East but also in the entire war. The war dragged on for another two and a half years, but it was now obvious that Hitler had made a fatal mistake in attacking the Soviet Union in the first place.

The defeat of the Germans at Stalingrad encouraged the partisans in the conquered parts of the Soviet Union, especially the Ukraine, to intensify the campaign against the invaders, and although the Germans assigned an increasing number of troops to cope with the attacks, local resistance could not be stilled. Then, five months after the Battle of Stalingrad, in July 1943, the Germans launched another offensive, which ended with a humiliating defeat in the Battle of Kursk (in southwest Russia). It marked the first time that Soviet troops beat the Germans in what had come to be known as a specialty of German commanders, 'mobile warfare', that is, heavy reliance on tanks and airplanes. In this battle, the Soviet commander deployed no fewer than 3,600 tanks and about 2,800 planes.

One reason for the Soviet success was that the Soviet Union had received a considerable amount of advanced equipment from Great Britain and the United States. After this victory, Russian troops moved quickly in pursuit of the retreating Germans. But the Russians were ordered to halt their offensive in the summer of 1944, just as they reached the Vistula river not far from Warsaw, Poland's capital. Stalin wanted to give the Germans ample time to defeat the Polish underground forces, which had been ordered by the Polish government in exile in London to stage an armed uprising. The government intended to demonstrate that it enjoyed a large following in Poland, and thus signal to the Soviet Union to think twice before installing a communist regime in Warsaw.

The Polish underground fought valiantly and kept the Nazis at bay for sixty-two days. But despite the ferocity of the fighting the Russians offered the insurgents no help, even after the West appealed to Stalin do so. He refused with the following comment to Churchill and Roosevelt: 'Sooner or later the truth about the group of criminals [i.e., the London Poles] who have unleashed the Warsaw adventure will become known to everybody.' Stalin directed his forces to avoid Warsaw and to capture Romania and Hungary instead, guaranteeing that these two countries would be absorbed into the Soviet orbit. Eventually, Russian troops resumed their march through Poland into Germany. When the war ended with the defeat of Germany in May 1945, the Soviet army was entrenched in six Eastern European countries, as well as in eastern Germany.

Stalin, as noted above, had strayed from Bolshevik orthodoxy on several ideological issues in order to arouse mass support for the war, but that does not mean that he had lost sight of his ultimate goal, the replacement of capitalism throughout the world with socialism. The most effective way to reach that goal, he believed, was to strengthen the Soviet Union and to extend its influence, first over its neighbors in Eastern Europe and then in other parts of the world.

His long-range strategy emerged during the war in his dealings with Western statesmen, in particular Prime Minister Churchill and President Roosevelt. Before the first conference involving the three leaders, Stalin dispatched Molotov in January 1943 to London and Washington to sound out the Westerners on two issues. Most important, when would the West launch a second front in Europe to relieve the pressure on the Soviet Union? Somewhat less important at that time, would Great Britain and the United States present a united front against the Soviet Union once Germany capitulated?

On the first question, the answer, much to Stalin's annoyance, was that an invasion of Europe by Great Britain and the United States could not be expected in the near future; they were simply not prepared to undertake such a major military operation. But on the second question, Molotov had good news for Stalin, who had feared all along that Churchill, a staunch opponent of communism ever since 1917, would influence Roosevelt to adopt a hostile stance toward the Soviet Union. The US president made it clear to Molotov that he and Churchill did not see eye-to-eye on all issues. For example, they differed sharply on the question of imperialism. 'There were all over the world many islands and colonial possessions,' Roosevelt told Molotov, 'which ought for our own safety to be taken away from weak nations,' and he considered Britain to be one of the latter. Roosevelt then elaborated on his strong anti-imperialist views, giving Stalin enough to go on to believe that he might be able to take advantage of the differences between the two Western leaders. He could now rest assured that when he met them he would not be in the minority, certainly not on all issues. Molotov also presented Stalin with detailed information on the politics of the advisers to the leaders of Great Britain and the United States.

At their first meeting, in Tehran in November 1943, Stalin gave a performance that impressed the two Western statesmen, both of whom had been briefed about the Stalinist system of rule. The dictator, who was used to issuing orders that his officials did not dare question, now posed as a simple and friendly man; he was courteous, spoke briefly on the issues of concern to him, and indicated that while he had strong opinions, he would not press them very hard. Nor did he appear to be too eager to ingratiate himself with the two Western statesmen. Only once did he offer a proposal that caused consternation; he suggested that as soon as the war was won the Allies should execute fifty thousand German officers, including the General Staff, who, he said, should be the first to be killed. When Churchill expressed shock, Stalin and his subordinates immediately tried to calm the prime minister by claiming that the Soviet leader had spoken in jest. All in all, Stalin gave the impression of being a reasonable politician with whom it would be possible to reach agreement on the many questions that would have to be settled immediately after the war. Both Roosevelt and Churchill left Tehran with a positive view of the Soviet dictator. Adam Ulam, no admirer of Stalin, concluded that Stalin's wartime diplomacy was 'dazzling'. The main decision of the conference related to the ending of the war: Germany would be required to agree to 'unconditional surrender'.

Almost a year later, in October 1944, Churchill, who in 1946 launched the Cold War by warning the West that Stalin was determined to export communism, went to Moscow to discuss the future of the Balkans. During one of his meetings with Stalin and his senior advisers, the prime minister offered Stalin the now famous 'percentage deal' that assured the communists a dominant position in southeast Europe. Churchill gave Stalin a piece of paper on which he had noted how the Balkans should be divided into British and Soviet spheres of influence. Churchill proposed the following: in Romania, the USSR would have ninety percent of the influence and Britain ten percent; in return, Britain would be granted ninety percent in Greece; in Yugoslavia and Hungary, the USSR would get fifty percent; in Bulgaria, the USSR would get seventy-five percent. Stalin examined the paper, and suggested that in Bulgaria, the USSR should have ninety percent. There was some quibbling and finally the statesmen agreed on the following changes: there would be a fifty-fifty percent division of influence in Yugoslavia, and in Bulgaria the Soviet Union would be granted eighty percent of the influence.

In February 1945, when it was understood that Germany would soon capitulate, the 'Big Three' met again, this time in Yalta, in the Crimea, in a summer palace where Russian Tsars had retired on their vacations. The Soviet Union had borne the brunt of the fighting and its army controlled Poland and much of Eastern Europe, making it difficult for the Western leaders to resist Stalin's demands. President Roosevelt was ailing – he died a few months later, before the cessation of hostilities – but in addition he had convinced himself that if the West was to succeed in influencing Stalin, he would have to be sharply critical of the British. At one point, he told the Soviet leader that the British were 'a peculiar people' who liked 'to have their cake and eat it too'. He was following the counsel of his main adviser on foreign policy, Harry Hopkins, who during the meeting sent the following message to the president when the discussion of reparations from Germany was under way: 'The Russians have given in so much at the conference that I don't think we should let them down.' Roosevelt had also told William Bullitt, the former ambassador to Moscow, that, contrary to his fears, he, that is, Roosevelt, had a 'hunch' that Stalin 'won't try to annex anything and will work with me for a world of democracy and peace'. The major concession by Stalin that Hopkins referred to was the Soviet leader's promise that free elections would be held in Poland and the Balkans.

In the end, the conference at Yalta turned out to be a major victory for the Soviet Union: its army would be permitted to remain in Poland, as well as in other European countries. In addition, territorial changes favored by Stalin would be implemented: parts of Poland would be annexed by the Soviet Union and Poland would be compensated with lands taken from Germany. In return, Stalin promised that within six months he would declare war against Japan and that he would join the United Nations, which was to be established to prevent future wars. But in an agreement kept secret, Stalin was promised that the Soviet

Union, together with four other countries – the United States, Great Britain, France, and China – would be accorded veto power in the Security Council, the most important and powerful committee of the United Nations. Thus, the Soviet Union was guaranteed a major role in international affairs.

Stalin emerged from the war with greater prestige than ever before. He received credit for having led the country to victory in a war that had seemed lost and for having expanded communism to cover vast stretches of Eastern Europe. The Soviet army was entrenched in Poland, Romania, Bulgaria, Hungary, and eastern Germany, and all of them would fall under the control of communists within a few years. In Albania, local forces, with the help of the Yugoslav army, formed a communist government, while in Czechoslovakia the Soviet Union maintained a strong presence, which enabled the communists to take power in March 1948. And in several countries in Western Europe, most notably Italy and France, the Communist Parties were so strong that it seemed possible that they would soon join the Soviet camp. But the Kremlin restrained the leaders of the French and Italian parties from attempting to take control of the governments in their countries because Stalin did not want to antagonize the West prematurely. It seemed as though Stalin's long-standing dream of expanding communism into the West would soon become a reality.

The victory over Germany had been achieved at a heavy price, and it would take the Soviet Union several years to return to the economic and demographic level it had reached in 1939. The country's loss in human lives ran to 7.5 million soldiers and somewhere between 6 and 8 million civilians. No country at war with Germany suffered losses anywhere near this scale. Geoffrey Hosking has estimated that the Soviet Union's losses in human lives were 'probably ... some forty times those suffered by Britain or some seventy times those suffered by the United States'. All these casualties, it should be remembered, came on top of those endured by the Soviet Union during the terror and purges of the 1930s. In 1939 the country's population had totaled about 194 million; five years after the war ended, in 1950, it had reached only 178.5 million.

In addition, much of the western part of the country, as well as such major cities as Kiev, Leningrad, and Moscow, had suffered enormous physical damage, reducing the availability of housing. Agricultural products became even scarcer than they had been before the war, since large parts of the most fertile lands had been occupied and ravaged by the German invaders. A few statistics will indicate the scope of the economic losses incurred by the Soviet Union; the grain harvest of 99.5 million tons in 1940 was reduced to 30 million in 1942 and 1943. During the same period the number of cattle declined by about one half. Eight years after the war, in 1953, the country still had fewer cattle than in 1916, when the population was much smaller (by about thirty million).

It was now also more evident than ever before that collectivization had been a colossal failure. The private plots of land, no more than two percent of all the land under cultivation, produced more than one half of the staples consumed by the Soviet population. At the same time, collective farmers struggled to stay afloat. If they wished to buy a suit – not even one of high quality – the cost was more than they earned in a year.

If the Soviet Union were to retain its status as a major power, its leaders would have to repair the damage inflicted on its economy during the 1930s and World War II and create one that could compete with the advanced economies of the West. This proved to be a herculean task.

9

Leader of a Great Power, 1945–1953

Once the war was over, many people in the Soviet Union hoped that their leader would continue the relatively moderate political and social course he had adopted during the conflict, when he needed all the support he could get. But it soon turned out that Stalin's moderation was a temporary ploy. Even before the final shots were fired, he reverted to his true self. He ordered whole nationality groups suspected of treason to be deported to the Siberian deserts. The Crimean Tatars and the Ingush-Chechens were shipped off without even the pretext of a judicial procedure to determine their guilt. Also, after the war ended, Stalin once again sent thousands of citizens whom he suspected of having in any way challenged his authority or betrayed the country to concentration camps in Siberia and the Far North. According to Isaac Deutscher:

> Their new inmates were officers and soldiers who had, as prisoners of war, spent dreadful years in German camps. No sooner had they crossed the frontier of their country than they were subjected to interrogation; and without being allowed even to see their families, they were imprisoned and deported. So were many of the civilians whom the enemy had mobilized in the occupied provinces for forced labor in Germany. They were all

branded as traitors: the soldiers for having disobeyed Stalin's orders, according to which they should not have allowed themselves to be taken in by the enemy; the civilians for having collaborated with the enemy. It did not matter that Stalin's orders had been impracticable, that millions of soldiers had been forced to disregard them, and that they had amply redeemed the 'breach of discipline' by the torment they had suffered in captivity.

If the government's ruthlessness was not quite on the scale of the terror in the 1930s, it was far-reaching and painful for many Soviet citizens. Moreover, there were no significant changes in the structure of the government. Stalin retained dictatorial power, all positions of influence remained in the hands of members of the Communist Party, and citizens were still imprisoned without due process of law. And on occasion, Communist Party members with a distinguished record of public service still incurred Stalin's wrath. The most famous case was that of Nikolai Voznesensky, who, after serving as Chairman of Gosplan and as Deputy Premier, was falsely charged with treason because he disagreed with Stalin on how to measure economic activity. He was secretly tried in 1950, found guilty, and immediately shot.

Stalin saw no reason to change the social and political order he had imposed on the country in the 1930s. In a speech delivered on 6 February 1946, about ten months after the defeat of Nazi Germany, he indicated that the military victory confirmed him in his belief that his ultimate political goal and conduct of affairs were correct. 'Our victory,' he declared, 'means above all that our social system has won ... our political system has won.' In that speech, he also announced that collectivism and rapid industrialization, his key policies in the 1930s, would continue to form the main elements of his economic program. In the field of culture, writers, composers, film directors, and painters were not treated as harshly as they had been before the war; but they were not permitted to publish, display their work, or have their music performed if it did not accord with the demands of the state. In short, the Stalinist regime of the 1930s was restored.

But in one important respect the Soviet Union had changed: it had been expanded into what some scholars have dubbed the Soviet Empire. In the Eastern European countries that had turned to communism, the Soviet Union deployed a significant number of its troops along with so-called advisers, who were often employees of the NKVD, to make certain that these states adopted a political order and economic policies that met with the Kremlin's approval. The one exception was Yugoslavia, which had been liberated from Germany by Yugoslav partisans under the leadership of Josip Broz Tito, and therefore was not beholden to the Soviet Union. As will be seen below, this independence helps explain the rupture between Yugoslavia and the Soviet Union in 1948.

Most of these territorial arrangements were ratified at the Potsdam Conference in July 1945, the last meeting of the Big Three, a group whose membership had changed since the Yalta Conference. President Roosevelt had died in April 1945 and was replaced by President Harry S. Truman, and Prime Minister Churchill was replaced by Clement Attlee, the leader of the Labour Party, which had won the national election held in Britain earlier that month. At Potsdam, Stalin again pretty much secured the approval of the West for all his demands: Germany was divided into four 'spheres of occupation', each to be occupied by either the USSR, France, Britain, or the United States. That arrangement satisfied Stalin's demand that Germany be so weakened that it would no longer pose a military threat. In addition, in accordance with agreements reached at Yalta, part of East Prussia was handed over to the Soviet Union and parts of Silesia and Pomerania were annexed by Poland, which yielded some of its eastern territory to the Soviet Union. Six to seven million Germans were expelled to the four zones of Germany to make room for the resettlement of Polish and Soviet citizens.

During the Potsdam Conference, on 24 July, President Truman informed Stalin that the United States had performed a test detonation of an atomic bomb, which not only opened up a new era in warfare, but also had a strong impact on relations between the Soviet Union and the West. Stalin did not seem to be perturbed or surprised. His spies probably had kept him abreast of the progress scientists in the United States were making in developing the bomb. But the announcement spurred the Soviet government to speed up its own efforts to create such a bomb, a move that later added to the strain in relations between the Soviet Union and Western powers.

By this time, an increasing number of statesmen in the West, who had been inclined to believe that Stalin had mellowed, were beginning to be troubled by his behavior. It now seemed clear that the Soviet Union was returning, in a slightly modified form, to its pre-war domestic policies and, more troubling, was taking steps to impose its system of rule on Eastern Europe. Before his death, even Roosevelt had begun to have doubts about Stalin's conduct. Roosevelt had adopted a conciliatory approach to Stalin at the Tehran and Yalta Conferences, in part because he hoped that his concessions would prompt the Soviet leader to be cooperative in establishing an international body to prevent future wars. But Stalin's actions early in 1945 suggested that he did not intend to maintain good relations with the West. He annoyed several Western leaders, including Roosevelt, by charging that during the last months of the war the United States and its allies had conducted secret negotiations for a peace treaty with Nazi leaders, which was not true. Then he offended the United States government by refusing to allow Americans to enter Poland to care for US soldiers who had been freed from German captivity by the Russian army. Shortly before he died, the president privately expressed doubt about the possibility of cooperating with the Soviet leader: 'We can't do business with Stalin. He has broken every one of the promises he made at Yalta.'

Churchill, who, despite his secret deal with Stalin regarding the Balkans, harbored deep distrust of communism, was the first Western statesman to sound a public warning about the course of events in Eastern Europe. On 5 March 1946, he delivered a speech entitled 'The Sinews of Peace' at Westminster College, a small college in Fulton, Missouri. Fulton was a village of seven thousand, but the attendance at Churchill's speech numbered forty thousand, and President Truman traveled all the way from Washington to introduce the speaker, two indications that an important pronouncement was expected.

One colorful sentence summarized the content of the speech: 'From Stettin in the Baltic to Trieste in the Adriatic, an iron curtain has descended across the Continent.' Eastern Germany, one sector of Austria, and six countries (Poland, Czechoslovakia, Hungary, Yugoslavia, Romania, and Bulgaria) were under Moscow's control, and in all of them the 'Communist parties, which were very small ... have been raised to preeminence and power far beyond their numbers and are seeking everywhere to obtain totalitarian control. Police governments are prevailing in nearly every case, and so far, except in Czechoslovakia, there is no true democracy.' Churchill reminded the audience that 'this is certainly not the Liberated Europe we fought to build up. Nor is it one which contains the essentials of permanent peace.' He did not believe that 'Soviet Russia desires war. What they desire is the fruits of war and the indefinite expansion of their power and doctrines.' Only cooperative efforts by the forces of 'the English-speaking Commonwealths' and the United States working together with the 'United Nations Organization' could muster the industrial, military, and moral power to provide 'an overwhelming assurance of security' against the encroachments of the Soviet Union. Many Westerners criticized Churchill for bringing up issues that were bound to divide the wartime alliance, but historians now generally agree that Churchill's speech marked the opening salvo in the Cold War, which was bound to break out sooner or later. In the West, the Soviet Union's influence over large areas of Europe and eventually also of other continents was considered by many not merely a military threat but also a threat to its civilization.

The Cold War lasted some forty-five years and ended with a conclusive victory by the West and the collapse of the Soviet Union. There were dangerous moments during that long period of hostility and on occasion it seemed that a military conflict was inevitable, but both sides shied away from what would have been a catastrophe for the world.

In March 1947, President Truman, no doubt influenced by Churchill's warnings, announced in a speech to a joint session of Congress that the United States would seek to halt the spread of communism in Europe and elsewhere by offering economic and military assistance to any country threatened with a communist seizure of power. He specifically had in mind the attempt by local communists to take over the government in Greece. He also urged Congress to supply funds and arms to Turkey, which was a factor in persuading the Turkish government to refuse the Soviets a base they coveted in the Turkish Straits. The Truman Doctrine, as the president's policies came to be known, was adopted by Congress and became a major deterrent to Soviet expansion. It also led some countries that had wavered between communism and democratic capitalism to opt for the latter.

In April 1948, the United States launched the Marshall Plan, which was designed to support the economic recovery of European countries from the devastation of World War II. As part of the program, the American government offered financial help to the Soviet Union, but Stalin decided against it on the ground that the purpose of the largesse was not to boost European economies but, rather, to undermine international socialism. In a retaliatory move, the Kremlin founded the *Cominform*, an international movement whose purpose was to synchronize the policies of the various communist movements in Eastern Europe and to provide support to Communist Parties in Western Europe. It was not as influential as the *Comintern*, which Stalin had dissolved in 1943 as a gesture of friendship to the West, but its existence was another indication of Stalin's resolve to expand the reach of communism. It soon became evident that the Soviet Union's rejection of the Marshall Plan was, economically, a huge mistake; during the four years of its existence the United States transferred about $17 billion (worth $160 billion today) to participating countries and it is generally regarded as a significant success in improving the economies of several European countries.

But Stalin's ideological commitments meant more to him than the economic well-being of the Soviet Union. In February 1948, the Czech government, which had consisted of a coalition of several parties, including communists, was overthrown and replaced by one dominated by communists. Early in May, the country was declared a 'people's republic', in effect a communist dictatorship. It was a move that deeply distressed many people in Western Europe and the United States, who remembered that in 1938 Great Britain and France had not come to the aid of the country when Nazi Germany seized control of it. Now the communists imposed their will on Czechoslovakia and again no one came to its rescue.

Late in June 1948, in protest against the Truman Doctrine and the Marshall Plan, Stalin struck back at the West in a somewhat peevish way by ordering a blockade of West Berlin, which was an enclave inside Soviet-dominated eastern Germany. No traffic could enter the areas of Berlin occupied by American, British, and French forces. Stalin thought he could starve the citizens of West Berlin into submission and in that way achieve one of two goals: Western countries would have to abandon Berlin altogether, which would be a major defeat for them, or they would be obliged to agree to abandon their plan of turning the parts of Germany occupied by American, British, and French forces into a single country allied with them against the Soviet Union. But the West remained adamant and in 1949 established the Federal Republic of Germany. More important, the Western powers outwitted Stalin on Berlin: they organized an amazingly efficient airlift to the city, which supplied the population in the western sectors with their basic needs. Desperate to avoid communist rule, the Germans in those sectors made many sacrifices to remain outside the Soviet bloc.

Stalin persisted in maintaining the blockade, and for an entire year he believed that the West would have no choice but to capitulate. When he realized that neither the West nor the Germans in their sectors would surrender, he changed course and ended the blockade. The entire operation turned out to be a major defeat for the Soviet Union. During the year of the blockade public opinion in Western Europe and the United States became more critical than ever of communism. That made it easier to bring about changes to strengthen the West: in April 1949, the North Atlantic Treaty Organization (NATO) was established.

Eleven European countries and the United States were the founding members of the organization. Its purpose was to serve as a warning to the Soviet Union that any attempt to expand its influence by military means would encounter forceful resistance. The United States maintained a significant military presence in Europe to shore up the forces of other members of NATO. Eventually, Turkey and Greece joined the organization, providing it with additional strength. NATO proved to be the backbone of 'containment', the West's overall policy vis-à-vis the Soviet Union for over thirty years. The goal of Western statesmen was to prevent aggression by the communists by warning them that the price would be so steep that it would be best to avoid recourse to force. Containment proved to be an effective policy: Western Europe remained in the democratic camp and although the influence of communism expanded in some regions of the world, it did not threaten the vital interests of the United States and its allies. And another world war was avoided.

In the meantime, late in August 1949, Stalin scored a triumph of his own that caused consternation in the non-communist world. The Kremlin announced that Soviet scientists had exploded an atomic bomb. It was a signal achievement and it meant that the Soviet Union, which had already enhanced its standing in the world by inflicting major defeats on the German army, was now the only country aside from the United States to be a nuclear power. And its prestige rose even more four years later, in 1953, when Soviet scientists exploded the country's first thermonuclear device.

The extent of anxiety that this development aroused in the West came to light only recently, on 27 October 2014, when the *New York Times* ran a front-page article entitled 'In Cold War, U.S. Spy Agencies Used 1,000 Nazis.' The central theme of the article read as follows: 'At the height of the Cold War in the 1950s, law enforcement and intelligence leaders like J. Edgar Hoover at the Federal Bureau of Investigation and Central Intelligence Agency aggressively recruited onetime Nazis of all ranks as secret, anti-Soviet "assets", declassified records show. They believed the ex-Nazis' intelligence value against the Russians outweighed what one official called "moral lapses" in their service to the Third Reich.' It had been known that former Nazis had been recruited by American officials, but the recently released documents show that the 'government's recruitment of Nazis ran far deeper than previously known and that officials sought to conceal those ties for at least half a century … Some spies for the United States worked at the highest level for the Nazis.'

In fact, American intelligence agents vastly exaggerated the Soviet Union's military might, either deliberately to enhance their importance or out of ignorance. In 1953, the Soviets had only one long-range bomber, the Tu-4, and its range was limited. It could fly all the way to the United States to drop bombs, but it could not return to the Soviet Union without refueling. More-over, Khrushchev revealed after Stalin's death that the plane was outdated, and several other long-range bombers produced in 1956 and 1957 did not survive their flight tests; they crashed. Khrushchev also divulged that an aircraft designer suggested that Soviet planes could bomb the United States and then land in Mexico, where they could refuel. To which Khrushchev responded: 'What do you think Mexico is – our mother-in-law? You think we can simply go calling any time we want?' Stalin came up with another way to bombard the United States: with intercontinental missiles, but their production was only incipient, and Soviet scientists pointed out that it would take years to develop them.

Realizing that they had no military options to counter the Western policies to safeguard Europe against communist expansion, Soviet leaders initiated a peace campaign in 1948 that sought to depict the United States with its large stockpile of nuclear weapons as warmongering. The campaign reached its climax with the Stockholm Appeal of 15 March 1950, allegedly signed by 500 million people (including all adults in the Soviet Union); it called for banning the atomic bomb. The campaign received a good deal of publicity, but it did not change the foreign policy of any major country aligned with the United States.

Although the successes of the Soviet Union in expanding its influence in Eastern Europe after 1945 were impressive, the process was not always smooth. The first instance of resistance to Stalin's expansionism took place in Yugoslavia, which, as already noted, had adopted a communist government under Marshal Tito, who had led an army of communist insurgents against the Germans and had seized power with little outside help. The Kremlin thought that the country would stand solidly with the Soviet camp. But when Tito, who stood solidly with the left but also professed nationalist leanings, wanted to annex the Italian port city of Trieste in 1945, Stalin refused to sanction the move because he wished to avoid conflicts with Western countries. The

Cold War had not yet started and he still hoped to expand his influence without antagonizing the West.

According to Milovan Djilas, a senior official in Tito's government, tensions between his country and Stalin's regime had actually surfaced as early as 1944, and they were grounded in moral rather than political differences. At that time, Djilas believed, as he put it, that 'the essential fact ... is the American ambition to dominate the world. This constitutes ... a menace even greater than fascism.' But Djilas was also deeply disturbed by the behavior of the Red Army when it invaded Yugoslavia in 1944; Soviet troops engaged in widespread looting and other crimes, and Soviet commanders 'were deaf to complaints, so the impression was gained that they themselves condoned the attacks and the attackers'. Tito and Djilas decided to raise the question with General Korneev, Chief of the Soviet Mission in Yugoslavia. The general responded to the query by shouting that he protested 'against such insinuations against the Red Army'. Four years later, in 1948, when the dispute between the Soviet Union and Yugoslavia had reached a climax, Stalin and Molotov dredged up the complaints Djilas had leveled against the Red Army, which the Soviet leaders considered offensive. At a public meeting in Moscow that Djilas attended, Stalin lashed out at Tito: 'Can't he understand it if a soldier who has crossed thousands of kilometers through blood and fire and death has fun with a woman or takes some trifle?'

Stalin's glib statement about the misbehavior of Soviet troops helps explain the extensive raping of women and looting by the Red Army when it entered Germany in 1945. The soldiers no doubt knew that they would not be punished.

At bottom, the conflict between the Soviet Union and Yugoslavia grew out of Stalin's growing hostility to Tito, who was trying to enhance his position by securing the leadership of a Balkan federation consisting of Yugoslavia, Bulgaria, and Albania. The historian Robert Conquest has suggested that Tito's ultimate goal was to become 'a sort of Balkan Stalin', which, of course, would have been unacceptable to the Soviet leader. He could not abide any rival to his preeminence in the socialist movement and he never doubted that he would prevail in any confrontation with the Yugoslav leader. During a discussion of the conflict, he told Khrushchev that 'I will shake my little finger and there will be no more Tito. He will fall.' In this instance, Stalin exaggerated his power, but in June 1948 he did succeed in persuading the Cominform to expel Yugoslavia and to move its headquarters from Belgrade to Bucharest.

Tito remained in power and also remained a committed Marxist, but he introduced relatively moderate economic and social programs that he claimed were modeled on Leninist principles. When Djilas published a book, *The New Class*, in which he argued that the Soviet Union was governed by a corrupt class with an insatiable appetite for power, the work struck Tito as sheer heresy, and he punished his former assistant with three years in jail. He also did not allow *The New Class* to be published in Yugoslavia; a Yugoslav edition finally appeared in 1990, five years before Djilas's death and ten years after Tito's. To a considerable extent, then, the rift between the Soviet Union and Yugoslavia resulted from conflicts between two leaders with strong egos, although the ideological differences sharpened after they parted company.

Apparently in an effort to prevent similar defections in other Eastern European countries under Soviet domination, Stalin ordered the governments in the satellites to move faster in collectivizing agriculture, to take strong measures to rein in religious institutions, and to place more restrictions on non-communist political organizations. Finally, Stalin urged the Communist Parties in Eastern Europe to conduct purges similar to those of the 1930s in the Soviet Union. It was not enough for Stalin that the governments in his empire subscribed to Marxist doctrines; they were also expected to establish the kind of political system that prevailed in his country.

One example will suffice: the dramatic trial in Czechoslovakia in November 1952, which appeared to many people at the time to be a throwback to events in Moscow in the mid-1930s. Fourteen leaders of the Czech Communist Party, including the General Secretary, Rudolf Slansky, were charged with having participated in a 'Trotskyite-Titoite-Zionist conspiracy'. The tribunal found all fourteen communists guilty; eleven were hanged in Prague thirteen days after the trial began, and three were given life sentences. Eleven of the accused were Jewish, which was widely interpreted as indicating that the Soviet Union would no longer support Israel. Initially, in 1948, when the state of Israel was founded, Stalin had been well disposed toward the new country on the assumption that it would side with the USSR against Western imperialism. But when Israel turned for allies to the West, the Soviet Union increasingly showered its favors on Arab countries, especially Egypt.

Although Stalin remained firmly in control of the Communist Party and the Soviet Union after the end of World War II, he showed signs of physical decline. He was in his mid-sixties and both his demeanor and his work habits had changed. Many people who saw him during this period noted that he had aged and that he now followed an unusual routine. By 1949, he rarely held formal meetings of party or government officials. He rose fairly late in the morning and worked at odd hours of the day and night. His subordinates had to adjust to his schedule.

Each day, his inner circle of advisers, consisting of Beria, Malenkov, Khrushchev, and Bulganin would show up at his apartment and invariably watch a movie or two – Stalin loved films, especially those that dealt with cowboys or with heroes of the Russian Civil War. At times, when there was a lull in the presentation of the films, the group would discuss some political or economic issue on which a decision was needed. At 1 or 2 A.M., Stalin would suggest that the group retire to his dacha for dinner. The guests always tagged along even when they were not hungry. Refusal to dine with Stalin would offend him, and that is the last thing his colleagues would have wanted to do. Before Stalin would take any food from a dish, someone else would have to taste it; he would not take a chance that it might be poisoned. The group drank a good deal, told jokes, some of them not suitable for polite company, and, if necessary, discussed a few matters of importance that needed Stalin's opinion, which invariably was the final word on the matter. The gatherings usually broke up by dawn.

Stalin no longer bothered to convene party congresses, which had traditionally been held every few years. Even the Politburo now met rarely. If consequential questions had to be resolved, it was up to Stalin to do so and he relied for advice on his dinner partners. In October 1952, he finally convoked a party congress, the nineteenth and the first one since 1939, but to the surprise of the delegates, his role in the proceedings was minimal. He was seventy-three at the time and no longer able, or simply did not want, to deliver the usual speech on the state of affairs that normally lasted several hours. He left that up to Malenkov, who occupied the position of Secretary of the Central Committee and was one of Stalin's favorite advisers. Stalin spoke for only a few minutes, and the accomplishments of the gathering were minor. The congress changed the name 'All-Union Communist Party (B)' to 'Communist Party of the Soviet Union', and that of the 'Politburo' to 'Presidium'. The Orgburo, which made major decisions on the selection of members to various party and government committees, was abolished altogether and its functions assigned to the Presidium.

Stalin's age may well have been the main reason for his silence, but it is also possible that he was so secure in his position as boss that the deliberations of elected party members simply did not interest him and, in any case, would have had little bearing on how the country was governed.

Stalin's family life, which had become dysfunctional in the 1930s, was virtually non-existent during his last years. His oldest son, Yakov, for whom Stalin had nothing but contempt, was no longer alive. He had served as an officer during World War II and was captured by German soldiers. The German High Command offered to exchange him for a German general held by the Soviet army, but Stalin refused to make the trade. His captors then executed him. Stalin had another son, Vasily, by his second wife. Vasily never quite settled on a career and was known as a heavy consumer of alcohol and also of various prohibited drugs. He joined the army during World War II, was rapidly promoted, fought bravely in several battles, and by 1946 had reached the rank of Lieutenant General. But after the war he again failed to establish himself professionally; he was a hockey aficionado and served in 1950 as manager of the Soviet Air Force's hockey team. In 1953, two months after his father's death, he was found guilty of having disclosed sensitive government information at a dinner party and was imprisoned until 1960. He died in 1962 at the age of forty-one of what was officially described as 'chronic alcoholism'.

Svetlana, Stalin's third child, was the one with whom the dictator maintained what one might call a normal relationship between parent and child, at least until her teens. In 1967, by which time she had escaped from the Soviet Union and moved to the United States, she published a book of memoirs, *Twenty Letters to a Friend*, in which she described her closeness to her father. True, he had not spent much time with her, but he made a point of seeing her fairly frequently and often sent her loving notes. All that ended in 1942 when Svetlana, at the age of sixteen, fell in love with Alexei Kapler, a film scriptwriter twenty-three years her senior. They saw each other several times, but it is not clear whether they consummated their love for each other. When Stalin heard of the affair, he fell into a rage. Not only was Kapler much older than her, but also he was a Jew and, as will be seen below, Stalin had a long history of prejudice against Jews. Stalin could not contain his anger as he shouted at her: 'You could not find yourself a Russian!' He then informed his daughter that 'Your Kapler is a British spy. He is under arrest!' Kapler was sent to prison for five years and prohibited from ever living in Moscow. When he violated that restriction in 1948, by going to the capital after his release, he received another prison sentence, this time to five years in a labor camp. Only after Stalin died in 1953 was he permitted to make Moscow his home.

At the time of her involvement with Kapler, relations between Svetlana and her father became estranged, and she never again managed to lead what most people would consider a normal life. She was married three times, twice to a Soviet citizen and once to an American, and had a four-year relationship with an Indian political activist. After severing her ties with the Soviet Union and settling in the United States, she met the architect William Peters, whom she married in 1970 and divorced two years later. Before that, she gave birth to a daughter, Olga, who made her home on the West Coast of the United States. Svetlana also had two children in the Soviet Union, where they remained after their mother moved to the United States. Svetlana's relations with them were strained, a source of much anguish to Stalin's daughter.

Svetlana's spiritual life was also turbulent. At birth, she was baptized into the Russian Orthodox Church, but her father was a passionate atheist. She did not refer to any discussions with her father about religious matters, but she seems to have found solace in religious belief. In 1982 she converted to Catholicism, and spent her last years, from 2007 to 2011, as a devout member of the church in the small US town of Richland Center, Wisconsin.

Svetlana was a troubled person but she was also intelligent and often insightful. The descriptions of people and events in the USSR in her autobiography throw light on Stalin's personality and the character of several of her father's close associates. Especially interesting is her account of her meeting with her father in 1947, when she visited him in Sochi. He impressed her as acting like an old man: 'He wanted peace and quiet. Rather, he didn't know just what he wanted. In the evening he viewed upbeat musical comedies like *Volga-Volga*; afterward he ate and drank late into the night.' This characterization of the aged Stalin resembles in some important respects accounts of other people close to him at that time.

But as the events in the Soviet Union during the last months of his life demonstrate, he had by no means lost interest in politics or, more important, his determination to rule the USSR according to his own lights. As Djilas put it after visiting Stalin early in 1948, the dictator was still 'stubborn, sharp and suspicious whenever anyone disagreed with him'.

The accuracy of Djilas's assessment of Stalin's personal traits became evident on 13 January 1953, when the government announced the uncovering of an ongoing plot by nine distinguished doctors, most of whom were employed by the Kremlin Medical Service. The allegations against the doctors were startling: they had killed Zhdanov, the former head of the NKVD, who had died in August 1948; they had passed secret information to foreign agents; they planned to kill leaders of the Soviet armed forces; and, more broadly, they were determined 'to wipe out the leading cadres of the USSR'. The announcement did not reveal why medical professionals would have committed themselves to mass murder. Nor has any document been found that indicated why Stalin charged the doctors with heinous crimes. But he took the proceedings against them with the utmost seriousness; he himself planned and supervised their interrogation. While the doctors remained in detention, the general view took hold that Stalin was gearing up for another purge on the scale of the trials of the 1930s. It seems plausible that Stalin feared that leading party officials had forged close ties with each other over the preceding fifteen years, a development that he might well have viewed as a threat to his authority.

Stalin may also have been motivated by another consideration. Seven of the nine doctors accused of planning to kill Soviet leaders by medical means had Jewish names, which led people at the time to fear that Stalin was planning a major action against Jews, such as deporting them to some distant regions of the USSR. As noted above, Stalin had already banished nationality groups he did not trust to Siberia, and the expulsion from Russia of Jews would not have set a precedent.

During most of his career as a Bolshevik activist, Stalin had not made anti-Semitism a major issue, but the evidence is strong that he disliked Jews intensely. His *Collected Works*, published in 1946, include comments he had made to the effect that the 'Mensheviks constituted a Jewish group' and that therefore 'it would not be a bad idea for us Bolsheviks to organize a pogrom in the party.' In 1905, he referred to the Menshevik leaders Martov, Fyodor Dan, and Axelrod as 'circumcised Yids' and called them 'cowards and peddlers'. During the last years of his life anti-Semitism seems to have become an obsession with him.

He now demonstrated his disdain for Jews more blatantly than ever before. In 1944–5, Ilya Ehrenburg and Vasily Grossman, two distinguished writers who had worked as reporters for the Red Army, tried to publish a book on the murder of millions of Jews by Nazis (often aided by Ukrainians). To their surprise, they ran into resistance from two censors, who did their best to prohibit the publication of *The Black Book*, as it was titled. Apparently, the censors were motivated by two considerations: senior officials insisted that Nazi atrocities were directed at Soviet citizens and not at any specific ethnic or religious group and therefore there was no reason to focus on the murder of Jews. Moreover, Soviet officials did not want it to be known that a fair number of Ukrainians participated in the slaughter of Soviet citizens. The book did not appear in Russian until 1980 and even then it was printed by a publisher in Jerusalem. Not until 1991 was a Russian edition printed in Kiev.

Another example of Stalin's hostility toward Jews was his order in 1948 to the Ministry of State Security to arrange the murder of Solomon Mikhailovich Mikhoels, the most distinguished actor on the Jewish stage in the 1920s and 1930s. During World War II, Mikhoels had served as chair of the Jewish Anti-Fascist Committee and in that capacity had traveled widely in Great Britain, Mexico, the United States, and Canada to garner support for the Soviet war effort. Three years after the war, Stalin convinced himself that while abroad Mikhoels had been involved in anti-Soviet activities, a totally baseless charge. After Mikhoels's murder, the police closed numerous Jewish institutions and arrested many prominent Jews. These events are generally considered to have marked the beginning of what has been termed 'official anti-Semitism' in the Soviet Union.

But Stalin's intentions in 1953 with regard to Soviet Jews remain a mystery that scholars have not been able to solve conclusively despite extensive archival research in Russia. The doctors still languished in prison when Stalin unexpectedly died. Any plans he may have entertained to crush an imaginary conspiracy and, as some scholars believe, to launch a new wave of terror similar to that of the 1930s had not been implemented. During the night of 1–2 March 1953, he suffered a hemorrhage in his brain, from which he never recovered. News of Stalin's illness, which incapacitated him, was not released until 4 March, hours before he died the next day.

According to reports of witnesses, Stalin's daughter and Khrushchev, Voroshilov, Lazar Kaganovich, Malenkov, and Bulganin cried when they received the news of the leader's death. Their distress is understandable. After all, Svetlana had been close to her father at one time, and the five men may have been overcome with grief out of fear for what the future held for them. They had all been Stalin's senior officials when the crimes of the 1930s were committed.

But the sorrow over Stalin's death ran deeper. At his funeral the crowds were so huge and so eager to be close to the speakers' platform that many spectators were crushed to death. In the past, similar disasters had occurred at the coronations or funerals of Tsars. More surprising, even in the prison camps established on Stalin's orders, many inmates wept. One prisoner said that he cried from shock, but that was not true of most who regretted the loss of their leader. Could it be that some wept because he had provided them with an all-embracing ideology that gave meaning to their lives and hope for a better future? As already suggested, ordinary Russians tended to look upon their ruler as their little father and with Stalin's death there would be no father, no one to tell the people what to do, or how to behave. Stalin had once said that 'Russian people want a Tsar', and he may have had a point.

Party leaders, and the press, mourned the deceased leader by recalling his achievements. At the funeral, his senior subordinates hailed him as 'the greatest military leader of all times and all nations'. Molotov acclaimed his contributions to economics and linguistics as 'new and most important discoveries of Marxist-Leninist science'. In the ensuing days, creative writers delivered encomiums that would surely have pleased the dictator. Konstantin Simonov, a well-known poet, playwright, and wartime correspondent, was at a loss to find 'words to render how insufferable our loss ... how we grieve for you, Comrade Stalin.'

But the new government, led by Malenkov, knew that Stalin was not the angelic figure depicted by these accolades. Four weeks after Stalin's death, the authorities announced that the doctors' plot had been a 'criminal fraud'. All the accused were declared innocent, but not all survived the ordeal of the interrogation; one of those charged with being a plotter had died and it is assumed that he may have succumbed while being tortured. About fifteen months after Stalin's death, in July 1954, Mikhail Ryumin, the Deputy Minister of Security who had been in charge of the proceedings against the doctors, was subjected to a secret trial, found guilty, and shot. Ryumin no doubt deserved severe punishment, but the judicial process could hardly have inspired confidence that the new government intended to abandon one of the harshest aspects of Stalinist rule.

Readers may wonder whether my depiction of Stalin and the system of rule he established is trustworthy. Could so self-centered, dogmatic, and cruel a person have reached the heights of power in Russia and remained there for twenty-four years? Is it possible that a man with his moral values could have gained the support of masses of people under his domination? Could a leader who fifty-three years after his death received a favorable rating of forty-seven percent in a poll of Russians have been guilty of so many crimes? It might be best to answer these questions by summarizing the comments made in a four-hour secret meeting at the Twentieth Party Congress late in January 1956, by Nikita Khrushchev, who had supported the state terror of the 1930s, had stood loyally at Stalin's side for over fourteen years, and at Stalin's death was appointed First Secretary of the Central Committee of the Communist Party of the Soviet Union. None of the delegates at the congress had expected to hear an account of Stalin's crimes, which they were sworn not to mention to anyone. It proved impossible to prevent leaks of a major address to over two thousand people on so explosive a subject. Early in March 1956, copies of the entire speech appeared in translation in the Western press.

Although readers who do not subscribe to communist dogma may not be persuaded by Khrushchev's explanation of the absence of effective resistance to Stalin's cruelties, there is no doubt that he delivered a remarkably candid and vivid account of the barbaric treatment of millions of Soviet citizens. The audience, which consisted of trusted officials of the Communist Party who must have known of the barbarities of the 1930s and 1940s even if they were not aware of all the gruesome details, was taken aback by the revelations; frequently the comment 'indignation in the hall' is interpolated in the printed version of the speech. Some members of the audience were so shocked that they became ill as Khrushchev recited details of Stalin's crimes – most of which are recounted in earlier sections of this book – and had to be assisted by ushers and colleagues in leaving the hall.

Khrushchev's aim, it must be stressed, was not to place the blame for the horrors of the Stalin era on Bolshevism. On the contrary, he held Stalin responsible for them and he insisted that the leader had distorted Marxist ideology by imposing on the country the 'cult of personality', a radical perversion of all that Lenin stood for. Khrushchev emphasized that Lenin had 'taught that the party's strength depends on the indissoluble unity of the masses, on the fact that behind the party follow the people – workers, peasants and [the] intelligentsia'. It was Lenin's firm belief that 'only he will win and retain the power who believes in the people, who submerges himself in the fountain of the living creativeness of the people.'

On the other hand, Khrushchev contended that Stalin had perverted and even abandoned the core principles of Leninism. In support of this contention, he informed the delegates that, shortly before his death, Lenin had warned (in his testament) that Stalin could not be trusted to serve honorably in a position of leadership. Stalin, Khrushchev continued, 'acted not through persuasion [and] explanation, but by imposing his concepts and demanding absolute submission to his opinions'. Whoever failed to follow the dictator's orders was 'doomed to be removed from the leading [party] collective and to subsequent moral and physical annihilation'. To dramatize this point, Khrushchev related the story of how Stalin badgered the Minister of State Security 'Comrade Ignatiev into forcing the doctors in 1953 to confess that they were plotting to kill many government leaders: "If you do not obtain confessions from the doctors," Stalin warned Ignatiev, "we will shorten you by a head."' This was greeted with 'tumult in the hall'. Toward the end of his speech, Khrushchev revealed that he suspected the dictator of harboring thoughts of another major purge toward the end of his life. Stalin, he indicated, 'evidently had plans to finish off the old members of the political bureau. He often stated that political bureau members should be replaced by new ones.'

Khrushchev's account of the terror was convincing because he did not limit himself to general charges against Stalin. For example, he provided precise figures – cited above in this book – on how many leading members of the Communist Party had been 'arrested and shot'. He accused Stalin of having 'so elevated himself above the party and above the nation' that he stopped paying attention to the views of other party officials and dealt harshly with anyone who opposed him. 'Confessions of guilt of many [party members] arrested and charged with enemy activity were gained with the help of cruel and inhuman tortures.' Khrushchev also accused Stalin of having failed to understand the threat that Hitler posed for Russia. 'As soon as Hitler came to power in Germany, he assigned to himself the task of liquidating communism,' but the leader of the Soviet Union did not take the necessary steps to prepare the country for its defense.

The weakest section of Khrushchev's speech was his attempt to explain why Stalin's crimes were abetted by so many people in high positions of authority, a fair number of whom were in the hall. 'Why didn't ... [the members of the Politburo] come out against the cult of personality?' Khrushchev offered a lame response to this query. He claimed that the leaders of the Communist Party 'viewed these matters differently at different times'; moreover, 'they did not know what the dictator was up to and all they knew was that there was not much they could do to stop him.' It would have required extraordinary honesty and courage on Khrushchev's part to provide a more convincing answer. In truth, the people at the highest echelon of the party were silent for two reasons: many did not disagree with Stalin's conduct of affairs, and those who did were afraid to speak out.

Nevertheless, Khrushchev's speech on Stalinism in 1956 was a brave endeavor to expose the evils of the twenty-four years of horrendous suffering of the Soviet people, but it would take much more than that to create a more humane society in which the people had the final say on how the country was governed. These were the hopes of many people after Stalin's death and even more so after the collapse of the Soviet Union in 1991. But such a political transformation of a country requires a citizenry educated to respect the rule of law and an economic system that supplies a decent living to a substantial majority of the population. The leaders of the Revolution of 1917 and their successors paid no attention to preparing the people for such a society. On the contrary, they dismissed the Western democracies as capitalist entities that ignored the wishes of the masses.

Epilogue: Stalin's Legacy

The most credible way to assess Stalin's legacy is to examine three related issues that were of paramount importance to him: his success in transforming the Soviet Union into a modern and well-functioning nation, a necessary precondition for turning the country into a socialist state; his success in changing the Soviet economy into a socialist order along the lines envisioned by Marx and Lenin; and, perhaps most important, the longevity of the political, social and cultural institutions he and his associates created.

There is no doubt that his policies changed the Soviet Union in fundamental ways: within about ten years, from 1929 to 1939, his initiatives succeeded in transforming the country from an essentially agrarian society into an industrial state and significant military power that after World War II extended its sway over much of Eastern Europe. And once the USSR acquired nuclear weapons in 1949 the country became a superpower, the only one that could pose a military threat to the other superpower, the United States of America. For over four decades, from 1949 until 1991, the two powers, one representing communism and the other capitalism, vied for supremacy in Europe, Asia, and the Middle East. It appeared to many people to be a clash of two world views, and at times it was not clear which one would prevail in what was known as the Cold War.

Even though Stalin's successors took far-reaching steps to abandon the system of terror that had accompanied Stalin's drive toward socialism, they were determined to preserve the Soviet Union both as a socialist state and as a superpower. Khrushchev emphasized these goals when he became the leader of the country in 1956. In an address in November that year to Western ambassadors at a reception at the Polish Embassy in Moscow, he warned: 'We will bury you.' Subsequently, he modified this prediction by indicating that he did not mean 'We will bury you with a shovel. Your own working class will bury you.' Throughout his period as leader (1956–64) he took numerous steps to continue the Cold War, which was part of the struggle to export socialism far beyond the borders of the Soviet Union.

But by the time Khrushchev left office in 1964, it had become evident that Stalin's achievements were far less solid than had been widely assumed. For one thing, discontent with subordination to the Soviet Union had burst into public view in several Eastern European countries. Yugoslavia severed its ties to the Soviet Union in 1948; riots broke out against Soviet control and against the communist system in East Germany and East Berlin in 1953 and Hungary and Poland in 1956; in East Berlin and Hungary, order was restored only after Soviet troops came to the help of local forces; massive unrest in Czechoslovakia in 1968 prompted the Soviet government to send troops to the country to disperse the turbulent crowds in the streets. And in 1980, unrest erupted again in Poland, which led to the creation of an independent and very influential trade union movement (called Solidarity) that stood in opposition to communism.

Moreover, in the 1960s it came to light that the economy created during the Stalin era was far less robust than Soviet leaders had assumed and claimed. In 1966, the government proudly announced that the country had entered the stage of 'mature socialism', but the data on economic development indicated that the standard of living under communism was much lower than in the capitalist United States and Western Europe. It also turned out that the standard of living of most citizens in the Soviet Union itself had not improved between the 1950s and 1966, largely because relatively little increase in the productivity of Soviet workers had been achieved. During the fifteen years from 1951 to 1966 the rate of increase in productivity of Soviet workers amounted to between forty and fifty percent of that of workers in the United States. In the view of many scholars in the West, the poor performance of workers under socialism had resulted in good measure from rigid central planning of the economy by officials in Moscow.

Economic conditions did not improve in the 1970s and 1980s, and public discontent became increasingly vocal. Again, one statistic is revealing; according to Professor Bruce Parrott of John Hopkins University, in 1970 there were fifty times as many computers in the United States as in the Soviet Union, a striking indication of how far the communist state lagged behind the West in up-to-date technology.

In 1985, a courageous reformer, M. S. Gorbachev, was elected General Secretary of the Communist Party, still the most powerful and prestigious political position in the Soviet Union. For six years, he valiantly attempted to loosen government control over the economy and political institutions, but his efforts at reform failed. The deficiencies of the economy and the discontent among citizens with their economic plight as well as with political institutions were too deep and too widespread for reform measures to succeed. Many believed that more radical measures were needed. At the same time, the minorities, who yearned for independence, showed increasing signs of unrest.

In 1991, discontent in the Soviet Union reached boiling point and, remarkably, the country collapsed into fifteen separate states with hardly a shot fired. Gorbachev still had sufficient forces to crack down on his opponents and the minorities, but he held back. He allowed the minorities to secede and he resigned as General Secretary.

The Russian Federation, or what is now commonly referred to as Russia, was the largest and most powerful of the successor states. It currently has a population of around 144.5 million, whereas the citizens of the Soviet Union had numbered more than 286 million. All the states in Eastern Europe that had come under communist domination after 1945 left the fold, and all now have capitalist economies. Two, Poland and Hungary, are headed by right-wing governments. Thus, the Soviet Union lasted seventy-four years, not a very long time for a political system that appeared to hold out so much promise at its founding. And the Soviet Empire, which included formerly independent states, lasted forty-five years.

The economy of the Russian Federation is a far cry from that of the Soviet Union. It is generally described as a market economy in which the so-called oligarchs, amply favored by the government, own huge companies and reap abundant profits, whereas the standard of living of most Russians is still low, well behind that of ordinary citizens in Western countries. Politically, the country is often described as a 'market democracy', that is, it has the trappings of democracy but amounts to an authoritarian form of rule, in which the President (Vladimir Putin for much of the post-communist era) is the dominant figure.

Early in his career, Putin was an officer in the KGB (Committee for State Security), and he has indicated that in his view 'the collapse of the Soviet Union was a major geopolitical disaster of the century.' He has taken various steps to reestablish Russia as a great power, but he has not succeeded in restoring the stature the Soviet Union enjoyed during Stalin's last years.

According to an analysis by Paul Sonne in the *Wall Street Journal* of 11 May 2015, Putin and his subordinates have adopted a cautious approach to the 'Soviet Union and its symbols ... that highlights ... Stalin's crimes but leaves room for its lionization'. The reason for this cautious public assessment of Stalin is that Putin's most devoted followers are divided in their views of the former leader: a fair number admire Stalin and many others cannot forget the terror of the 1930s.

But among the public at large, the assessment of Stalin has become far less unfavorable over the past sixteen years. In

2000, forty-three percent of Russians who participated in a poll viewed him with dislike; by 2015, that number had shrunk to twenty percent. Although only a few people, including Putin, deny Stalin's tyranny, a growing number praise him for having stimulated economic growth and, apparently even more so, for his leadership during World War II, which saved the country from Nazism and established it as a foremost power in international affairs. In an article in the *New York Times* of 13 March 2016, Alec Luhn, a journalist based in Moscow, reported that in a poll published in the Russian Federation in January 2015, fifty-two percent said that Stalin 'probably' or 'definitely' had 'played a positive role in the country'. The intelligentsia, especially those who live in Moscow, form the backbone of those who 'abhor' Stalin, and they constitute a minority of the country's population.

Memorial, a Russian human rights organization, has expressed deep concern over this attitude toward Stalin, but so far its warnings about the dangers of public praise for a leader who committed so much evil have not been heeded by a substantial number of citizens. Many human beings, it seems, tend to forget the pernicious policies of political leaders and remember only their achievements, however fleeting they may have been. Victor Erofeyev, a novelist, has argued that widespread repudiation of Stalinism is not likely in the near future. Touching on a theme first advanced by Hellbeck and Halfin and discussed above, Erofeyev has suggested that 'when Stalin dies in the soul of the last Russian, then you can say that our country has a future.'

The latest poll can be construed as a compliment to the man who led the Soviet Union for twenty-four years. But it is surely reasonable to assume that Stalin, a man of enormous self-confidence as well as a fervent believer in socialism, would have been profoundly distressed at the thought that his legacy would be a country that no longer championed socialism and that as a result of the breakup of the Soviet Union in 1991, lost half its population. Moreover, even though President Putin has sought to restore the country's status as a world power by seizing Crimea from Ukraine and by intervening in Syria's civil war, he has so far not succeeded in lifting the Russian Federation to the level of power and prestige it enjoyed during Stalin's last years as leader of the Soviet Union. It was then one of the two great superpowers, the other one having been the United States. In fact, countries in Eastern Europe – such as, for example, Poland, Romania, Hungary, and Czechoslovakia – that used to be in the Soviet sphere of influence are now independent and tend to consider themselves to be allied to Western powers. It is unclear how the efforts of President Putin to reestablish Russia as a superpower will turn out. But at this moment it does not seem likely that the Eastern European countries or the Western powers will make it easy for the Russian Federation to once again rise to the level of a superpower. Only a few decades after Stalin's death his legacy would seem to be rather meager.

Bibliography

Alliluyeva, Svetlana. *Twenty Letters to a Friend*. London, 1967.

Arendt, Hannah. *The Origins of Totalitarianism*. New York, 1951.

Bullock, Alan. *Hitler and Stalin: Parallel Lives*. New York, 1992.

Cohen, Stephen F. *Bukharin and the Bolshevik Revolution. A Political Biography, 1888–1938*. New York, 1973.

Conquest, Robert. *The Great Terror: A Reassessment*. New York, 1990.

—— *The Harvest of Sorrow: Soviet Collectivisation and the Terror-Famine*. New York, 1985.

Deutscher, Isaac. *Stalin: A Political Biography*, 2nd ed. New York, 1967.

Djilas, Milovan. *Conversations with Stalin*. New York, 1962.

Fainsod, Merle. *How Russia Is Ruled*. Cambridge, MA, 1963.

Fitzpatrick, Sheila. *Everyday Stalinism: Ordinary Life in Extraordinary Times: Soviet Russia in the 1930s*. New York, 1999.

—— *On Stalin's Team: The Years of Living Dangerously in Soviet Politics*. Princeton, NJ, 2015.

—— 'Revisionism in Retrospect: A Personal View', *Slavic Review*, Vol. 67, No. 3, Fall 2008, pp. 682–704.

—— 'Revisionism in Soviet History', *History and Theory*, Vol. 46, No. 4, December 2007, pp. 77–91.

Gellately, Robert. *Stalin's Curse: Battling for Communism in War and Cold War*. New York, 2013.

Getty, J. Arch. *Origins of the Great Purges: The Soviet Communist Party Reconsidered, 1933–1938*. New York, 1985.

Guderian, Heinz. *Panzer Leader*. New York, 2002.

Halfin, Igal and Jochen Hellbeck, 'Rethinking the Stalinist Subject: Stephen Kotkin's "Magnetic Mountain" and the State of Soviet Historical Studies', *Jahrbücher für Geschichte Osteuropas*, Vol. 44, No. 3, pp. 456–63.

Hellbeck, Jochen. *Revolution on My Mind. Writing a Diary under Stalin*. Cambridge, MA, 2006.

Hosking, Geoffrey. *The First Socialist Society: A History of the Soviet Union from Within*. Cambridge, MA, 1993.

Khlevniuk, Oleg V. *Stalin: New Biography of a Dictator*. New Haven and London, 2015.

Knight, Amy. *Beria: Stalin's First Lieutenant*. Princeton, NJ, 1993.

Koestler, Arthur. *Darkness at Noon*. New York, 1941.

Kotkin, Stephen. *Stalin, vol. I, Paradoxes of Power, 1878–1928*. New York, 2014.

Laqueur, Walter. *The Fate of the Revolution*. London, 1967.

Lewin, Moshe. *Lenin's Last Struggle*. London, 1969.

Ludwig, Emil. *Leaders of Europe*. London, 1934.

Martin, Terry. *The Affirmative Action Empire: Nations and Nationalism in the Soviet Union, 1923–1939*. Ithaca, NY, 2001.

Montefiore, Simon Sebag. *Stalin: The Court of the Red Tsar*. London, 2004.

—— *Young Stalin*. New York, 2005.

Nove, Alec. *An Economic History of the USSR 1917–1991*, 3rd ed. London, 1990.

Overy, Richard. *The Dictators: Hitler's Germany and Stalin's Russia*. New York, 2006.

Pipes, Richard. *The Russian Revolution*. New York, 1990.

Ribbentrop, Joachim von. *The Ribbentrop Memoirs*. London, 1954.

Schapiro, Leonard. *The Communist Party of the Soviet Union*. New York, 1960.

—— *Totalitarianism (Key Concepts in Political Science)*. London, 1972.

Service, Robert. *Stalin: A Biography*. Cambridge, MA, 2005.

Snyder, Timothy and Ray Brandon, eds. *Stalin and Europe: Imitation and Domination, 1928–1953*. New York, 2014.

Solzhenitsyn, Alexander. *One Day in the Life of Ivan Denisovich*. New York, 1963.

—— *The Gulag Archipelago, 1918–1956*. New York, 1974.

Souvarine, Boris. *Stalin: A Critical Survey of Bolshevism*. London, 1939.

Stalin, Joseph. *History of the Communist Party of the Soviet Union (Bolsheviks): Short Course*. New York, 2013.

—— *War Speeches, Orders of the Day and Answers to Foreign Correspondents during the Great Patriotic War, July 3, 1941 – June 22, 1945*. London, 1946.

—— *Works*, Volumes 1–13. Moscow, 1952.

Taubman, William. *Khrushchev: The Man and His Era*. New York, 2004.

Trotsky, Leon. *My Life*. New York, 1960.

Tucker, Robert C. *Stalin as Revolutionary, 1879–1929*. New York, 1974.

—— *Stalin in Power: 1928–1941*. New York, 1990.

Ulam, Adam B. *A History of Soviet Russia*. New York, 1996.

—— *Stalin: The Man and His Era*. Boston, 1989.

Volkogonov, Dmitri. *Stalin: Triumph and Tragedy*. London, 1991.

Wolfe, Bertram D. *Three Who Made a Revolution: A Biographical Study*. New York, 1955.

Index